The (Magic) Kingdom c

The (Magic) Kingdom of God

Christianity and Global Culture Industries

Michael Budde

Westview Press
A Member of the Perseus Books Group

Copyright © 1997 by Westview Press, A Member of the Perseus Books Group

Published in 1997 in the United States of America by Westview Press, 5500 Central Avenue, Boulder, Colorado 80301-2877, and in the United Kingdom by Westview Press, 12 Hid's Copse Road, Cumnor Hill, Oxford OX2 9JJ

Library of Congress Cataloging-in-Publication Data
Budde, Michael L.
    The (magic) kingdom of God : Christianity and global culture
industries / Michael Budde.
        p.   cm.
    Includes bibliographical references and index.
    ISBN 0-8133-3075-0 (cloth) — ISBN 0-8133-3076-9 (pbk)
    1. International business enterprises—Religious aspects—
Christianity.   2. Advertising.   3. Mass media.   4. Marketing.
5. Christianity and culture.   6. Identification (Religion).
7. Evangelistic work.   8. Christian education.   9. Catholic Church—
Membership.   I. Title.
BR115.E3B83   1997
261—dc21   97-17603
                                                                        CIP

The paper used in this publication meets the requirements of the American National Standard for Permanence of Paper for Printed Library Materials Z39.48-1984.

10   9   8   7   6   5   4   3   2   1

Contents

Acknowledgments

One of the better things about writing books, I've discovered, is that you meet some of the nicest people in the process. In researching, writing, and revising this manuscript, I've found myself able to impose on the generosity of large numbers of people who have been willing to read, critique, encourage, and challenge my work.

I've benefited from the insights of many people. Joseph Komonchak, Albert Borgmann, Michael Warren, Stanley Hauerwas, Larry Bennett, Eric Hanson, Patti Goff, Stan Howard, Bob and Cindy Bernstein, and Pat Callahan all read substantial sections of this book in manuscript form. Each made important suggestions, corrections, and observations. Whether they were helping me avoid embarrassing errors, showing where my prose failed me, or giving me a sense of what sections worked well, they enabled me to say what I wanted with more clarity, brevity, and consistency.

My first experience with a commercial publisher landed me in the midst of editorial musical chairs at Westview Press; that it was acquired by Rupert Murdoch's conglomerate makes for no small irony, given the subject of my book. I am grateful to Gordon Massman, who initially signed me for this book. More recently, I've benefited immensely from the advice and encouragement of Laura Parsons. Like the editor of my first book, Laura is a first-rate professional who is also a Chicago Cubs fan. I'm not quite sure what to make of this correlation, but it continues to intrigue me.

Bob Brimlow, a philosopher at St. John Fisher College in Rochester, New York, managed to work through every chapter and draft of this manuscript. He gets high marks for endurance, if not for knowing when to refuse a request for help. He proved to be a demanding but fair critic, a source of encouragement and comic relief; he also has the capacity to consume more coffee than any human being I have ever met. He won't live long at this rate, but I'm grateful he's been my friend for at least a while.

Some of the ideas in this book receive real-life confirmation in the day-to-day struggles and triumphs of my parish. Sacred Heart Church is an

African-American Catholic congregation on the "wrong" side of the river in Joliet, Illinois. Its members and pastor, Father Dick Bennett, have made my family and me feel accepted and challenged. At this church most people understand that the gospel is a dangerous and subversive call, one that shakes the foundations of business as usual and the priorities of the powerful. On a good day, Sacred Heart gives a taste or a sample of what God had intended the Church to be. I wish everyone could know a Church like this one.

I owe personal thanks to my family: my parents (Dick and Marilyn), my brothers (Dan, Tom, and Kurt) and their families, and my grandmother (Dorothy Meyers). I owe more than I can express to my wife, Terri, and our children, Rachel, Sean, and Zachary.

Together they help me learn about the Christian life—and how much I have yet to learn about practicing what I preach—and why it is important to continue to "seek first the Kingdom of God."

Michael Budde

1

Following Jesus in a
Distracted Age

Once upon a time, I was hired as a consultant for a public-policy arm of a state-level Catholic bishops' conference. The bishops, according to the institution's staff people, wanted to engage in rededicated efforts to confront the realities of poverty in their state.

What the church bureaucracy had in mind was something on the order of a new lobbying initiative in the state legislature or perhaps an expert conference on poverty in the state.

I told them that they should attempt to take every Catholic in their state on an intensive retreat, with follow-up programs upon their return. Nothing the Church could do would benefit poor people more, I argued, than to energize, inspire, and ignite the passion of larger numbers of the faithful. Without attempts to "convert the baptized," in William O'Malley's phrase (1990a), the stranglehold of self-interest, isolation, and religious indifference would continue to throttle church attempts to deal seriously with poverty in a global capitalist order.

My advice, to put it gently, was unappreciated. I was fired. They had an experts conference. As far as I can tell, poverty in their state remained indifferent to their efforts.

Catholicism as a "Discipleship Church"?

Whenever and wherever Christianity has been an engaged, radical force for justice and human freedom, it has been because enough persons and groups in the church were passionate about the gospel, were deeply invested in the role of "disciple." They have been committed to making as their own, as best they can under their circumstances, the choices, affections, and praxis first of Jesus of Nazareth, then of other exemplars of the faith. These exemplars themselves, whether prophets, mystics, social radicals, or church reformers, were similarly seized or given over to the grand narratives of Yahweh's covenantal love in the Hebrew Scriptures and/or Jesus and his evocations of the Kingdom of God.

Whether one confines the scan to modern examples—movements against slavery, apartheid, the arms race, the exploitation of women, economic justice—or goes back further in history, an absolute requisite for Christian witness in the world is the presence of faith-based *passion*. The notion of passion, as will become apparent, is an underlying concept for much of this book. It ties together questions of religious formation that must move from background to foreground if we are to have churches worth preserving in the contemporary era; it points to the central narrative of Christian experience (the passion of Jesus) from which we derive our most potent insights into the life, mission, and message of the Anointed One; and, in the form of disordered and trivialized passions (a product of the cultural ecology of our time), we in the advanced industrial world find ourselves less able to sustain *any* life-forming narrative that is recognizably Christian, indeed, less able to be "passionate" about anything. I suggest that a Christianity drained of passion is no Christianity at all, the ultimate oxymoron, a pasty and thin gruel "neither hot nor cold," and thus rejected by God (Rv 3:15). Indifference to the gospel, more than heresy, aberrant interpretations, or partisan politics, is the greatest danger to the church today.

Calls for more, rather than less, religious passion must strike Western ears as perverse, if not outright dangerous. The so-called modern age, born in the aftermath of interreligious wars and insecurity, can be seen as a thoroughgoing attempt to defuse religious passions, to render them harmless and unworthy of cultivation. In a world in which Christians still kill one another, in which narrow movements of "Christian inspiration" threaten human freedom and seek state power for their causes, revitalized and renewed Christianity must indeed seem threatening. And, indeed, the revitalized, passionate Christianity I seek *is* threatening to the world as it is, although not for the reasons usually assumed. But before making that point, I must make clear what I do *not* mean by Christian passion.

First, Christian passion is not uniform in its expression; it is not to be confused with William James's notion of religious "enthusiasm," his category for ecstatic/charismatic experiences. Charismatic phenomena may— or may not—be signs of authentic Christian passion as I conceive of it. They are not identical with it.

Second, Christian passion is not a fanatical close-mindedness; it does not coerce consciences and behaviors. Rather than seek power in the worldly sense of domination, strength, and lethal means, it inspires people to live a radical reversal in which service is privileged over being served and "success" is measured in ways often considered bizarre by outside judges.

Third, Christian passion is not a substitute for, or in opposition to, human reason and the intellect. It does not privilege irrationalism, emotivism, or anti-intellectualism; rather, the sense of Christian passion I advocate stands prior to, but not independent of, the exercise of human reason. It orients and motivates individuals and groups to exercise their intellectual and cognitive gifts in the service of the Kingdom and Christian discipleship. To the extent that these goals are of transcendent significance, intellect and reason become more, not less, important to individuals and groups who hope to take on the mind of Christ.

The more I have come to reflect on the notion of passion in Christianity, the more fertile the metaphor becomes—pulling together ideas and practices, texts and interpretive communities, churchly and worldly concerns. Several things come to mind that will be explored throughout subsequent chapters.

Hans Frei and others have argued that the passion accounts in the New Testament historically have constituted the central narrative of Christian experience. Indeed, it seems fair to say that it was the specific, historical *passions* of Jesus—for the poor and exploited, for a way of being that affirms life and not death, and against wealth, power, and privilege—that led the powers that be to set in motion his passion/execution. The "eclipse of biblical narrative," in modernist scriptural study and scholarship, detailed by Frei (1974), in turn has meant marginalizing the particulars of Jesus' ministry and praxis as orienting guides for Christian life. The consequences of this move have been considerable.

As evidenced in the synoptic Gospels, the passion of Jesus radically scales down all other desires, subordinating them to the central imperatives of proclaiming and living the new reality of the Kingdom. It identifies the idolatry that is misplaced passion, that puts the "natural" categories of cult, family, property, and purity above the imperative "Follow me" (Lk 5:27; 14:26–7; Mt 10:35–6). The willingness to let go of inferior passions and loyalties, to "die to" lesser goods, is a sign that passion for the gospel is taking root in believers and in communities (e.g., Lk 18:28–30).

Christian passion seeks to do, to live, and to be all *ad majorem Dei gloriam* (AMDG) ("to the greater glory of God"), in the words of the Jesuit

motto. For some members of the Church, this "AMDG" leads to martyrdom or a highly visible witness in the world; for others, it may manifest itself as the "little way" of St. Therese—living a life of obscure vocation,
perhaps caring for sick relatives, comforting the lonely, or "praying at all
times" (Lk 21:36), if such is all that circumstances allow. In ways large or
small, one is to do as much as can be done to live Jesus' way, while always
seeking to change those circumstances in ways that enable a more comprehensive practice of discipleship. The church is the community called to
live as an alternative community, the group in the world that empowers,
enables, and encourages its members toward a more complete, more passionate embrace of the gospel and its way. It is here, as part of the church,
that the humble and limited practices of discipleship become enlarged by
being part of a collective project. The Eucharist is the sacramental call to
do as Jesus did, to affirm the community's efforts to continue and intensify their efforts in this regard.

In this view, one test of the integrity of the Church is whether it is content to baptize the limited practices of its members, instituting a minimalist, legalistic interpretation of Christian life and practice or whether it cel-
ebrates the positive limited practices that exist while acting as a source of
encouragement, imaginative experiments, fraternal/sororal correction, and
collective movement along the Way of Christ. None of this is a matter of
Pelagianism, or works-righteousness, or Pharisaism (Lk 11:37–46): perfection in the Christian life is beyond human capabilities, and accom-
plishment and pace matter less than direction and constancy.

One major obstacle to the renewal of more passionate expressions of
the Catholic tradition lies in the endurance of "dual ethic" thinking—the
notion that, although certain individuals might be called to "heroic" expressions of gospel discipleship (the saints and martyrs, for example), such
a standard cannot be made normative for all believers. Particularly after
the accommodation with the Empire in the fourth century, two classes of
Christians emerged: an elite (almost always clerics or members of religious orders) whose socialization in the faith was considered crucial (and
from whose ranks most "heroic" exemplars emerged); and the great majority of the baptized, who were thought incapable of living lives of gospel
quality beyond minimalist expectations. This circumstance differs significantly from the practice of the pre-Constantinian church, in which baptism was considered an act of great significance, to be conveyed only after
long preparation and formation, and a covenantal step involving high expectations and mutuality. Dual ethic assumptions are a central element of

what I have elsewhere described as "loose" theories of the church—in which the similarities between the gospel and non-Christian ways of thinking and living are emphasized and in which being a Christian involves few obligations or loyalties that might conflict (except incidentally) with those privileged in the larger realms of power and influence (e.g., soldiers, capitalists, heads of state, patriots, citizens, revolutionaries) (see Budde 1992, pp. 33–4, 93).

The relative neglect of the religious and spiritual formation of the vast majority of believers during Christendom was justified by several dubious assertions of a theological and anthropological nature. The "simple people" were often thought to be "naturally religious," hence not requiring the expenditure of significant resources on their religious formation; being "simple" in social terms, the assumption that most were "simple-minded," and thus to be dictated to, seemed to follow almost inevitably. Also important were theological notions derived from the doctrine of Incarnation that held that since revelation builds upon (rather than opposes) the precepts of natural law accessible with unaided reason, concentrating religious resources on future leaders would still leave the great unwashed with those religious insights naturally available to them.

What "formation" of the laity that did occur in Christendom was often partial, incomplete, starved for resources, and designed not to interfere with the Constantinian bonding of religious and sociopolitical power— hardly the stuff to encourage manifestations of the Christian message in close continuity with those of the pre-establishment church. What Christendom represented instead was a "Christian ethos," built by force, represented in architecture and public art (among other things), as a substitute for intensive, gospel-centered formation. Intended or not, the effects of the dual ethic have been profoundly deradicalizing and alienated from the ecclesiologies of the New Testament and patristic eras. This explains at least some of the huge gaps between gospel values and the practices of Christianity in "Christian" Europe, Latin America, and elsewhere where the dual ethic has been determinative of church practice.

Such is not meant to disparage the sincerity of those whose faith is so described. Indeed, one can only marvel, with gratitude, at the depths to which the gospel has been internalized and lived in those parts of the Church left underserved and devalued by dual ethic thinking. For all that, it is still true that the gospel begins, for all of us, as a word from the outside—a set of stories, roles, and choices that do not spontaneously and randomly emerge across the time and space of history. Christianity is a *conveyed* tradition, one that is refashioned on the road, but one in which it matters if the versions conveyed are shallow, distorted, or drained of passion, or are life-engaging and capable of rearranging one's "natural" priorities and passions. In practice, it has never been an all-or-nothing thing, of course—even denatured, minimalist versions of the faith retain subversive potential and memories. Nevertheless, the dual ethic—poorly grounded in Scripture, better understood as a legacy of the Constantinian captivity of the Church than as a universally valid norm—remains an internal obstacle to revitalizing the Church's sense of mission and commitment.

Fortunately, some trends within Catholicism are pushing against the double-standard counsels of the Christian life. Most notably, the Church's renewed theology of baptism, which sees the sacrament as binding all—equally—in service to Jesus' mission on earth, undercuts much of the theological ground from beneath minimalist readings of popular discipleship. The more profound understanding of baptism, reflected especially in the Vatican II documents and the renewed Rite of Christian Initiation for Adults (RCIA), has implications not fully explored or accepted by the hierarchy; nevertheless, this enhanced view of baptism, with a more comprehensive set of entitlements and obligations, is a development that brings change and controversy in its wake.

Catholic Ecclesiology and a
Passion for Discipleship

It isn't a new idea, but I believe the primary purpose of the church is, and should have always been, to make saints. Its purpose isn't to be just a social service agency, nor to sponsor art for art's sake, nor to provide "meaning" and consolation to holders of power and privilege. Other movements can and do perform these sorts of things, often better than the church. What the church can and must do, what it alone can do, is make room for the Spirit within human hearts, to inspire individuals and groups to follow the example of Jesus of Nazareth. Anything less is to confuse byproducts with objectives, to be less than we are called to become, to trade the terrifying, adventurous birthright we inherited through baptism for inferior goods. Although I believe that certain social "goods" often emerge from the church when it is true to its own calling, those goods are derivative and dependent upon prior attention to the religious tasks of the church. Seeking the "goods" while neglecting the groundwork was the mistake of Protestant liberalism, which sought to legitimate Christianity as socially "useful" even while its "religious" underpinnings eroded from neglect and the impact of modernist rationalism.

As Church we are called, I argue, to become disciples of Jesus, to help one another take on the mind and heart of Christ, and to live our every-day lives in ways that reflect the choices, priorities, and dispositions of Je-sus as narrated in Scripture. Such a vision of Christian purpose requires a degree of religious passion and conviction that mainstream ecclesiologies (Protestant and Catholic) have sought to marginalize. We cannot engen-der the degree of conviction and fidelity to the gospel our era requires by working through unchanged church self-understandings and structures. We need to rethink our notions of church as *mission:* What is it we are supposed to be doing? and church as *community:* How are we to organize ourselves and move together in pursuit of the mission left us by Jesus through the Holy Spirit?

In Christian ecclesiology, one could construct an interesting genealogy stretching from Ernst Troeltsch's *The Social Teaching of the Christian Churches* (1913), Max Weber's *The Protestant Ethic and the Spirit of Capi-talism* (1905) through H. Richard Niebuhr's *Christ and Culture* (1951), to Avery Dulles's *Models of the Church* (1974). Troeltsch and Weber, and later Niebuhr (to a lesser extent Dulles), did much to establish as normative the distinction between "church" and "sect" types in theories of the church. To Troeltsch and Weber, sects—small, particularistic, demanding in their ex-pectations for believers' conduct and involvement—represented a notion of church that seemed to guarantee social marginalization, withdrawal from public concerns, and excessive "otherworldliness." The church type, in contrast, was more pluralistic in composition, allowing for a wide range of involvements, and better suited to influence politics and public con-cerns in a responsible manner.

I have elsewhere discussed at some length the ideological biases in favor of the status quo, of assumptions of strong continuities between secu-lar/Western and Christian values, that inhere in privileging the "church" model (and demonizing anything considered "sectarian"). The sect cate-gory works its rhetorical magic by insisting upon a very narrow definition of politics and public involvement (strongly state- and violence-centered) and by assuming that the church-type's minimalist interpretation of the gospel is truer both to the text and the "needs" of modern societies (Budde 1992, pp. 30–7). Using these categories, a boatload of theologians and

ethicists have sought to protect mainstream Catholicism from more demanding ecclesial visions with the assertion that while discipleship-style
(read "sectarian") practices might be tolerable for fringe groups, the
Catholic Church (in capital letters) is, by its very nature, too broad, too
grand, and too big for that. Catholicism is meant to be a "big tent" for all,
and "sectarian" demands represent steps backward to withdrawal into the
much-despised "Catholic ghetto."

A partial and interesting exception here is Dulles, a Jesuit scholar from
a patrician East Coast family. His *Models of the Church* was a touchstone
for most subsequent discussions about ecclesiology in the Catholic tradition. The influence of H. Richard Niebuhr is evident throughout Dulles's
book, along with the church/sect binary therein. In the years after 1974,
however, while continuing to develop the themes and topics that made
him one of the more influential American Catholic ecclesiologists of his
time, Dulles began exploring the relevance of more radical ecclesiologies
for Catholicism.

Two more recent works in particular stand out in this development. In
A Church to Believe In: Discipleship and the Dynamics of Freedom (1982)
Dulles developed the notion of discipleship—much as I have discussed it
thus far—and showed how it was a view consistent with Church history
and contemporary scriptural scholarship. When a new edition of *Models of
the Church* was published in 1987, Dulles added a final chapter, titled
"The Church: Community of Disciples," in which he outlined how the
discipleship model corrected and integrated the other postconciliar models he had identified in the first edition.

Dulles's work suggests that, far from being an alien import into the
Catholic world, movements to instill greater passion, commitment, and
"discipleship" are both appropriate and necessary. According to Dulles,
"Jesus did deliberately form and train a band of disciples, to whom he
gave a share of his teaching and healing ministry. 'Community of disciples' is precisely what Jesus undoubtedly did found, and once we recognize
this fact we can apply to our life in the Church many of the gospel pas-
sages dealing with discipleship" (1982, p. 8).

Further,

> the concept of discipleship makes it clear that each member of the Church is
> under personal obligation to appropriate the Spirit of Jesus. Church mem-
> bership, so conceived, is neither a passive acceptance of a list of doctrines,
> nor abject submission to a set of precepts, but rather the adventure of fol-
> lowing Jesus in new and ever changing situations. The Church may be

viewed as a community of followers who support one another in this challenging task. (Dulles 1982, p. 10)

Once the idea of Church as the gathered followers and disciples of Jesus is admitted, the New Testament sections on discipleship take on immediate, and personal, relevance. The call to discipleship, as Dulles notes, is "an imperious one" that "overrides all other concerns and obligations." Taken seriously, it means

> a break from the world and its values. In the Synoptic Gospels, especially, we see discipleship as involving a total renunciation of family, property, income, worldly ambition, and even personal safety. The disciple, in the ideal case, forsakes all other security, making a total commitment to Jesus and the kingdom. (Dulles 1982, pp. 8–9)

The obvious impossibility of such a lifestyle (except for "heroic" individuals) is evidence, to some Christian ethicists, of the inadmissibility of discipleship as a legitimate vision for the entire church. To me, what the impossibility of "perfect" discipleship suggests is that the role of disciple is one to be pursued only as part of a believing community—it is not *meant* to be an individualistic yoke upon the shoulders. Rather, the properties of discipleship, while always realized incompletely and imperfectly, apply both to communities and to persons-in-community.

The notion of the church as a gathering of disciples does indeed mark off the claims of church from those of "the world"; this is a major weakness, according to critics, and one of its best features in my view. If adopting as one's own the praxis, priorities, and affections of Jesus (as derived from the New Testament) condemns one to minority and peripheral status in the world, then perhaps what needs to be interrogated is the dominant notion that Christianity could *ever* have underwritten secular power relations without prostituting its heritage.

As Dulles indicates, Christian discipleship implies training, emulation, and processes of formation—none of which happens automatically or easily in "the world."

> In order to remain a Christian one must take a resolute stand against the commonly accepted axioms of the world. For this reason it cannot be taken for granted that the great majority of those baptized in infancy will grow up convinced Christians. Young Catholics, if they are to become true disciples, must undergo a demanding course of induction, equipping them to profess

the full faith of the Church in a secularized, neopagan society. They must develop a sense of solidarity, cemented by affective relationships with mature and exemplary Christians who represent Christ and his way of life. The Church cannot perpetuate itself except through a long chain of discipleship. (Dulles 1982, p. 11)

Dulles is far from the only voice within contemporary Catholicism calling for a more committed (in my terms, passionate) embrace of discipleship as the Church's focus. The concept shows up in some of the writings of Pope John Paul II (e.g., *Redemptor Hominis*, 1979, pp. 89–90) and the U.S. Catholic Bishops (although the latter retreat from the implications of the metaphor almost immediately in their major pastoral letters of the mid-1980s; see Budde 1992, pp. 86–93). Many of the finest works on Christian discipleship, Dulles observes, have been written by Protestants, and at various times Protestant churches have "practiced discipleship to the point of martyrdom" (1982, p. 15).

Obviously, I believe certain substantive theological and ethical conditions follow more easily from narrative/discipleship conceptions of the church than do others. Making a Christian case for "democratic capitalism" and for killing becomes much more difficult, if not implausible, under these conditions. Yet these are, and should be, matters to be discussed and debated within the church, provided that the language of faith is not forced to surrender to imperatives to be more "realistic," "relevant," or "acceptable" to non-Christian powers (Cuddihy 1978). The "narrative turn" in theology is not a recipe for fundamentalism or authoritarianism, does not presume only *one* correct interpretation of the stories of Jesus, and does not presume that all portions of Scripture are equally binding or to be read as having equal purchase on church conduct (Hauerwas 1981, pp. 70, 108–9). What narrative theology does, as an admittedly nonfoundational approach to theology (see Ochs 1993; Tilley 1995; and Hauerwas, Murphy, and Nation 1994), is free the church to take its own values and commitments seriously, to be different in the world, and to tell its stories without being embarrassed by their specific, local, Jewish, and particularistic roots.

For Catholics and other Christians to become more passionate about being church, they must realize how much in-house work is necessary in order to *disagree* appropriately, much less derive common agendas. One debates the various possible personal implications of the Sermon on the Mount differently within a community that sees the gospel and its "Follow me" as determinative for individual and group faithfulness; one cannot even *discuss* the issue in a church that has a priori decided that the particulars of Jesus' praxis and preaching must be bent to the "realities" of wielding and guiding secular power—and hence are largely irrelevant for church life (except for those "heroic" individuals).

Social Theory, Political Economy, Culture, and the Church

One of the most liberating consequences of the dethronement of behaviorist and positivist epistemologies in social theory is that scholars can finally admit the obvious—that we explore problems we care about, that we want our work to serve normatively contested goals, and that passion and commitment are preconditions for (and not barriers to) important intellectual work. This is how I situate my own academic efforts, in this book and elsewhere.

All scholarship, in other words, is polemical, in the sense of being concerned with persuasion and a preference for some interpretations/practices over others. This acknowledgment of the intrinsic partisanship of scholarly production is no license for intellectual laziness, oversimplification, or the systematic production (and destruction) of straw men and women. Rather, one should be *more* rigorous, more relentlessly self-critical, and more diligent when investigating matters about which one cares deeply.

Most scholarly production is intended for a definable audience or set of audiences, and this book is no exception. I hope it to be a contribution to the lives and work of other people for whom the radical renewal movements within world Christianity (especially within Catholicism) are sources of hope and evidence of spiritual vitality. For all their flaws, I continue to believe that such movements—which include the Catholic Worker and Catholic peace movements, some of the various forms of liberation and feminist theologies, and the anti-authoritarian resistance movements of Eastern Europe—represent a more legitimate, discipleship-oriented manifestation of the priorities, intentions, and practices of Jesus of Nazareth than do their more theologically accommodationist, less practically demanding predecessors and competitors. Although I make no secret of my theological preferences, I nonetheless conceive of my work as an offering of service to the entire church.

In addition, what follows may also be of interest to persons concerned with intellectual questions regarding international political economy and culture. No doubt it will also interest persons opposed to the movements I support. It may also be of interest to persons with less easily pigeonholed interests.

Choosing to identify oneself as a "Catholic scholar" or a "Christian scholar" in the 1990s is a decision not made lightly, nor without awareness of the multiple ambiguities implicit in the term. The decision to speak first to the Church (and not to larger, non-Christian political and social audiences) may strike some people as an unseemly violation of the rules of academic discourse, where the only audiences that count are those of state policymakers, one's academic peers, and other groups wielding considerable secular influence or power. For others, the notion of "Catholic scholar" seems as oxymoronic as "military intelligence" or "jumbo shrimp"; the former concept must exact a lethal toll from the latter.

The decision to work as a Catholic or Christian scholar is, in my view, defensible on multiple grounds. It has never been obvious to me why other audiences or communities of reference (one's country, academic discipline, or political hierarchy) should be viewed as any less limited or any more legitimate than the church. Certainly, as I read recent history, the Catholic Church has kicked the habit of killing as a way of maintaining its order and privileges (the same cannot be said for states); its tradition of reasoned investigation and concern for holistic scholarship need not be embarrassed by comparisons with the Enlightenment's intellectual progeny; and as the carrier and imperfect manifestation of the revolutionary, prohuman message that is the gospel, it seems a no less worthy repository for human hope and effort than the various ideologies, techniques, and pretensions of the modernist era. One need not agree with my positive, but critical, assessment of the church (as it is and as it should be) to admit the possibility that the prevailing competitors for human loyalties (nation-states, professional cliques, corporate benefactors, etc.) are not obviously more deserving.

Several years of playing the academic journal-submission game has convinced me that what I do is irretrievably antidisciplinary. It is too theological for the social science journals, not theological enough for the theological publications. Instead of settling for the Procrustean solution (what do you chop off when you want to weave together things that the disciplines say must be kept compartmentalized, if not altogether separated?), I continue to do what I do and hope that the extended canvas of a book-length manuscript will make the disciplinary trespassing seem more rhythmic, or at least comprehensible. Although I do not pretend to the depth and breadth of John Milbank, his *Theology and Social Theory* (1990) stands as one example of how such efforts appear when done well.

Like many others, I have been among those scholars who have sought to focus the attention of the academic world and its many audiences on matters of religion and their impact on social, political, and economic life. The study of religion and politics (broadly understood) has, after decades of relative neglect, enjoyed something of a minor renaissance over the past two decades.

With reference to the Catholic Church as a social and political force, the list of topics in recent years has been diverse. From Central America to Poland, liberation theology to the theology of democratic capitalism, the fall of communism and debates on sexual ethics, anti-authoritarian church movements in the Philippines and Korea, the church as a force for redemocratization in Brazil and Chile—the list seems endless, so numerous have been the connections. Observers and partisans, clerics and critics—nearly all have been impressed by the breadth and depth of religiously grounded activism and dispositions concerned with matters of power, freedom, and just order. As I plowed my own furrow in this field, two related questions forced themselves into my work.

First: As someone trained in political economy, I am well acquainted with matters of "reproduction" when speaking of a given political-economic order, for example, the construction and perpetuation of a labor pool, the consolidation and renewal of capital, the ongoing challenges of legitimating a given distribution of power and influence. What I became more aware of in the course of writing my first book was the way in which students of the church and politics ignored (or assumed away) matters of "religious reproduction." Most scholars, myself included, have too often assumed that whereas the particular involvements of the Christian community may vary according to time, place, and circumstance, the existence of that community is itself relatively unproblematic: there has been, and will continue to be, a "Church" that more or less resembles the body of Christ as we have known it. Through the training of children, the initiation of converts, and the ongoing education of adults, the re-creation of the church itself is not fundamentally called into question by matters external to itself except in circumstances of outright physical or social extermination (as attempted, for example, in Albania; even there, such efforts were ultimately unsuccessful). In its treatment of ecclesiology as both a theological and sociological category, my first book (Budde 1992) considered some of these matters but incompletely.

Second: I have learned much from the work of Eric O. Hanson, whose book *The Catholic Church in World Politics* (1987) observes that whatever power the Catholic Church wields in today's world is ultimately a reflection of its cultural (not economic, military, or political) power (1987, pp. 5–9). I worked with that assumption for several years before finally asking the obvious question: If the Church operates primarily as a cultural actor in the contemporary world, how is it affected by those actors who are *most* dominant in the exercise of cultural power? After a while, I came to identify as "most dominant" the global, trans-sectoral "culture industries" that account for the vast majority of the world's output of shared images, stories, songs, information, news, entertainment, and the like. How does the Christian movement, especially the Catholic community, move and act among the trees of the global culture industries, whose importance to the current operation of global capitalism is attested to by critics and defenders alike?

When combining these two questions, I found that my earlier work, and that of most of my colleagues, had ignored the present and future impact of global culture industries on matters of religious formation, education, and community mission. In a sense, we had focused on the flowering of the plant without noticing changes affecting the nutritional elements of the soil. While we may continue to debate endlessly among ourselves the Christian case for or against capitalism, for or against liberal democracy, we are assuming that the preconditions for "forming" a Christian, and later a Christian case for *anything*, are more or less a given, more or less a constant in the equation.

Not all within the Catholic world have been oblivious to such considerations, of course. In particular, the alarms have been sounded first and most loudly by some of the people involved in transmitting and "reproducing" the Christian tradition: the religious educators, the CCD (Confraternity of Christian Doctrine) teachers, the theorists and practitioners of spiritual formation. Upon the overworked shoulders of religious educators and catechists may rest even the possibility of *any* Catholic presence (much less a "passionate" one) in the much-discussed "postmodern" world.

The basic argument of this book is as follows: The cultural environment associated with the latest era of capitalism, dominated as that environment is by the global culture industries, presents new and imposing barriers (beyond those typical of earlier eras) to the formation of deep religious convictions. This should be as troubling for conservatives in the church who seek a principled affirmation of democratic capitalism as it is for those of us who find the gospel a permanent call to resistance of all forms of political, economic, and social domination. What is at risk is not any particular interpretation of the gospel or the tradition of the church but the capacity to think, imagine, feel, and experience in ways formed by the Christian story.

The next two chapters describe and situate the changes in the world political-economic system that increase the importance of cultural phenomena in the ongoing operation of that system. Drawing concepts from the "regulationist school" of political economy (e.g., Amin 1994; Lipietz 1987), as well as from other sources, these sections deal with jargon-infested matters of globalization, postfordism, and postmodernism; for-profit culture industries as wielders of "cultural power" in global capitalism; and the export (from what used to be known as the First World to Third World regions) of techniques and institutions that attempt to shape cultural practices and dispositions in specific, determinate directions. In these chapters, I hope to make ideas from contemporary political economy and social theory useful to people concerned about the church; "disciples," more than most people, need to understand the "signs of the times" in order to fulfill their mission in the world. While I have tried to make these concepts and processes understandable to a general audience, the intellectual terrain nonetheless remains rocky in spots.

Chapter Four offers a theory of religiosity and the construction of faith-based sensibilities that derives from various "postliberal" scholars across the disciplines. Chapter Five identifies the primary obstacles to Christian formation thrown up by the operation of some of the major culture industries. Chapter Six surveys the treatment of culture industries thus far by some major actors in the Catholic Church and a few major Protestant voices. These assessments are themselves evaluated, as are mainstream efforts in religious education and formation in advanced capitalist cultures.

The final chapter offers some reflections on how the church might better respond to the challenge of global culture industries and the world they create around us. Although such thoughts must of necessity be provisional, I would feel remiss without offering what suggestions I have for pastoral strategies designed to continue the church as a radical movement committed to the discipleship norms of Jesus.

Why Culture Matters in
the World Economy

Not long ago, if you wanted to understand the "real" ways of power worldwide, your field of study was fairly clear: pay attention to states, armies, and weapons; measure wealth, production capabilities, and prosperity. It was never really as simple as that, of course, but one derived a certain sense of security from assuming it was.

In this world of "real" power and influence, matters of culture headed for the back rows, if not out the door entirely. The realist and neorealist traditions in international relations ignored culture; the old-line Marxists reduced it to more important economic relations; and the rest of mainstream scholarship seemed to blow with the winds of fashion (is "traditional culture" an obstacle to development or an aid to it? The modernization folks, for example, have managed to take both sides of the question in succession, stepping on their own toes in the process). Although exceptions sneaked to the surface on occasion, overall the bulk of international political economy (IPE) scholarship dealt with "culture" as a remainder category at best, a repository for all the ill-fitting parts, inconvenient or ambiguous features that might detract from one's preferred explanation for the "real" processes of political and economic power.

Within the past two decades, matters of international political economy and culture have experienced a period of getting (re)acquainted. Some of the ensuing literature has pointed to the culturally bounded nature of foundational intellectual concepts (e.g., Campbell 1992; Walker 1992; Der Derian 1992). Others have highlighted the impact of patriarchal assumptions in structuring notions and perceptions related to power and influence (Enloe 1990, 1993; Murphy 1996).

Beginning only slightly before this resurgent interest in culture by political economists, the academic world also saw one of its periodic revivals of interest in the social impact of religion. The confident predictions of irrevocable secularization, of the withering of religion as a socially potent force, now seem as dated as starched shirt collars and fedora hats. Radical religious challenges to established relations of political and economic power emerged throughout the world beginning in the 1960s—in the Americas, Eastern Europe, the Persian Gulf, the Middle East, and elsewhere. As perhaps the archetypal "cultural" phenomenon (Paul Tillich's claim that religion *is* culture strikes me as too strong, however), "religion" clearly needs to be reckoned with in any discussion of the interaction of political economy and culture.

In an earlier work (Budde 1992), I attempted to do just that—consider the interactions, aided by a world-systems perspective, of a worldwide religious phenomenon (Roman Catholicism) with transnational capitalism. Several interesting insights—particularly involving the central significance of ecclesiology, to which I will return in later chapters, emerged from that project; however, the limits of the world-systems approach proved formidable, even as I attempted to correct for its deficiencies in dealing with culture generally and religion in particular. The patriarch of world-systems thinking, Immanuel Wallerstein, has only lately begun to make room for cultural considerations (1991); his appreciation for specifically religious matters remains inadequate. The neglect of culture and religion is not peculiar to Wallerstein or his school, of course; one competing statement of "globalization theory," for example, pays virtually no attention to such matters (Ross and Trachte 1990).

The broad argument I make in this book is as follows: Matters of cultural transformation, contestation, and (re)construction should move from being peripheral IPE concerns to a place nearer to the center. Not only will attempts to understand a number of worldwide political-economic transformations now well underway be incomplete without attempts to situate cultural factors, but analysts who fail to recognize the increased importance of the cultural strategies, tools, and objectives of key transnational actors will fail to identify new arenas of domination, contestation, and resistance.

More specifically, I argue that for the primary actors of transnational capitalism—private global firms—matters of cultural production are among the key factors in the expansion and consolidation of capitalism's next phase. This next phase is one driven by information, communications, and knowledge-based innovation and competition in a global (or at least regional, transnational) market. This much-ballyhooed transformation to a global economy depends in important ways on the relatively successful propagation of corporate-driven discourses, identities, and worldviews.

Finally, I argue herein that, alongside the more conventional "politics of interest" played by corporate actors in the public realm, transnational firms are now major players in a contested "politics of identity"—a struggle to define or affect self- and group perceptions in ways congenial to profitability, regularity, and social control. No longer limited to advanced capitalist countries, the corporate struggle for identity is a global one in which cultural resources and practices are fought over, co-opted, and restructured to fit the needs of transnational firms. Those same resources— religious, intellectual, normative, artistic, and more—are also the raw materials for new and emerging oppositional strategies and movements which do not necessarily cleave along neat class or national lines.

If these claims are more or less on target, the implications for the Christian churches and other religious communities are enormous. It is less a matter of presenting new problems for the church to deal with in its conventional ways; more fundamentally, the capacity of the church to survive with its core values intact is called into question. The global utilization of "culture" by transnational firms has radically altered the environment within which the church exists, first in the advanced industrial regions but increasingly in Third World contexts as well. This new cultural environment, unlike anything the world or the church has experienced before, increasingly undermines the preconditions for religious formation and praxis in the contemporary world. This should be as troubling for religious "conservatives" concerned about matters of sexual and personal morality as for religious "progressives" concerned with social justice and equity. Whatever capacity each has to bring their concerns into contact with the world may well dissolve under the corrosive effects of the cultural ecology now emerging.

A New Stage of Capitalism?
Regulation Theory and Neostructuralism

Within some political economy circles, debate continues on whether contemporary capitalism has entered a qualitatively new era (a position held, for example, by Mandel 1975; Aglietta 1979; Harvey 1989; and Ross and Trachte 1990) or merely a predictable cyclical shift within an unchanged capitalist system (the dominant world-systems theory view; e.g., Chase-Dunn 1989, pp. 54–70). While it is not clear that these two positions always lead to fundamentally dissimilar practical conclusions, the dispute is an important one likely to continue in the future.

Although much of my own thinking owes a debt to the world-systems school, it seems that there is clearly *something* different and important going on, particularly as one delves deeply into the cultural aspects of globalization. Capitalism is not new in the 1990s, but discerning its stable and variant features (and how they interact) remains an important theoretical and practical matter. In this, I find useful several concepts derived from the "regulationist school" of political economy, a heterodox blend of Marxist, institutionalist, and Polanyian assumptions (see Elam 1994, p. 57). While regulationism is not up to the job of serving as an all-embracing framework, capable of providing answers to all questions of international political economy and culture (much less to those posed by Christian concerns), it does highlight key relationships helpful in exploring many of those questions.

The regulationist school, in turn, is part of a larger family of IPE approaches described as "neostructuralist" by its practitioners. This approach, according to Ronen Palan and Barry Gills,

> asks how global processes interact with other processes of state/societal transformation occurring at many other levels of the world system . . . The first-order questions of neostructuralist approaches to International Relations [for example] are on the order of how state/society transformation at level A is affected by and in turn affects the transformations at level B and C, and so on. *It is the transformative processes themselves that are placed at the center of analysis.* (Palan and Gills 1994, p. 7)

While neostructuralism is a set of ideas in dialogue with world systems and dependency theories, "the essence of neostructuralism lies in the conviction that there are inherent limitations in the capacity of global or international patterns to create totalizing systems" (Palan and Gills 1994, p. 7).

Neostructuralism criticizes organismic, unitary conceptions of the state, whether such issue from the realist tradition in international relations or from neo-Weberian attempts to "bring the state back in." The state is to be disaggregated, deprivileged, and denied status as an actor with "needs," "goals," or a unique agenda. As Palan and Gills conceive of the state, "it is not an 'it'" (Palan and Gills 1994, pp. 4, 6).

Neostructuralist approaches draw attention to the degree to which individual choices (by firms, persons, etc.), although not "determined" by extrinsic structures, are nevertheless limited and framed by structures and relations:

> Thus, every practice and social relation figures within a concrete totality that is always already given and that determines that relation as its condition of existence . . . Though all relations contribute to the constitution of social reality, every singular practice takes social reality . . . for granted. This is what may be called the "ecological paradox": for although the socioeconomic space is a product of practices, it appears, however, as somehow externally given for each individual practice or interaction. (Lipietz 1994, p. 25)

Both regulation theory and neostructuralism represent attempts to confront anew the levels-of-analysis problems that plague international political economy: How, for example, do global and national/regional/local processes affect one another? How are transformative processes articulated within a given social space and across social spaces?

Regulation Theory as a Neostructuralist Approach

> The aim of the early French regulationists was to develop a theoretical framework which would encapsulate and explain the paradox within capitalism between its inherent tendency towards instability, crisis, and change, and its ability to coalesce and stabilize around a set of institutions, rules, and norms which serve to secure a relatively long period of economic stability. (Amin 1994, p. 7)

The orthodox Marxist "answer" to the interplay between the tendencies referred to by Ash Amin was the base/superstructure model. While never a complete picture of Marx's own thinking on this topic, the superstructural institutions (law, schools, etc.) "functioned" to contain the disintegrative impact of economic processes, helping to stabilize the system as a whole. The model is rightly criticized for its functionalism, its strong tendency toward economism, and a host of other vices.

Although regulationist-inspired approaches focus on the same problem as do the old-line Marxists, the differences between them are usually substantial. For the former, the capacity to find a stable fit between processes of capital accumulation and institutionalized forms of social stability cannot be assumed a priori; it is often an ad hoc, error-ridden, and historically contingent process. Moments of alignment may be relatively brief in historical terms and do not have within them the seeds of a predetermined successor era. Regulationists periodize capitalism by the features typical of these episodic harmonizations; consequently, they identify different "eras" within capitalism, where other scholars (with a longer time frame) see only "business as usual" (Chase-Dunn 1994, pp. 95–6).

Constructing a relatively stable context of some duration for capital accumulation involves an articulation between a *regime of accumulation* and a *mode of regulation.*

A regime of accumulation, according to Amin, refers to a set of regularities at the macroeconomic level that enables a stable, relatively coherent process of capital accumulation:

> It includes norms pertaining to the organization of production and work (the labour process), relationships and forms of exchange between branches of the economy, common rules of industrial and commercial management, principles of income sharing between wages, profits and taxes, norms of consumption and patterns of demand in the marketplace, and other aspects of the macroeconomy. (Amin 1994, p. 8)

A mode of regulation, in turn, is the "set of internalized rules and social procedures which incorporate social elements into individual behaviour" (Lipietz 1987, p. 15). It consists of formal and informal rules, cultural habits, and institutional behaviors that frame social relationships and make possible the reproduction of capitalism. Modes of regulation are built up through state policies, cultures of consumption, industrial codes, rules of negotiation and bargaining, social expectations and the like (Amin 1994, p. 8). In this usage, regulation is much broader in scope than is a focus on "governmental regulation" of economic activity.

The "fit" between a regime of accumulation and a mode of regulation does not emerge automatically, nor is it permanent. It would be "a big mistake" to assume that regulatory frameworks are designed in accord with a preexisting master plan, or an elite blueprint, or by a self-aware dominant class (see Lipietz 1992, p. 7). They are products of trial and error, experiments that manage to "work" for some extended period of time (Lipietz 1987, p. 15).

The most recent extended era of sustained capital accumulation has been described as "Fordist" by several authors (the term derives from Gramsci 1971). Elements of Fordism were visible early in the twentieth century, but the system did not fully consolidate until after the Depression and World War II. The Fordist era is commonly periodized as running from 1945 until around 1973.

Fordism's regime of accumulation included mass production techniques joined to Taylorist forms of labor control (e.g., "scientific management," technology utilized to enhance worker output, docility, and surveillance); polarization between skilled mental workers and unskilled workers; and increasing mechanization, leading to rapidly rising productivity and a higher ratio of capital goods per worker. Workers, in exchange for acceding to managerial prerogatives regarding investment and technological innovation, saw some portion of productivity increases paid to them as rising real wages. Consequently, major firms enjoyed stable levels of profitability and operated at or near full capacity in most years (Lipietz 1992, pp. 6–7).

The mode of regulation under Fordism included social legislation on minimum wages and collective bargaining; welfare state policies "which meant that wage-earners (indeed, the whole population) remained consumers even when they were prevented from 'earning their living' through illness, retirement, unemployment or the like"; and the expansion of commercial and consumer credit free from the constraints of gold reserves (Lipietz 1992, pp. 6–7). Consumerism as an ideology and lifestyle solved the "realization problem" (profits aren't "realized" until someone buys the product) as the steadily increasing output of factories was purchased by workers receiving steadily rising real wages.

The tense but stable labor-capital-state balance of Fordism did not emerge easily, but rather was the "outcome of years of struggle"—a struggle which involved, among other things, the defeat after World War II of resurgent, radical working-class movements in countries including Japan, West Germany, Britain, France, the United States, and the Low Countries (Harvey 1989, p. 133).

Although the United States was the dominant actor in the Fordist era, Fordism as a regime was international in scope. It came to some countries as a result of American occupation and reconstruction policies (Japan), via the post-1945 upsurge in American corporate investments abroad, or via imitation by countries that saw Fordist principles as necessary to compete with the Americans (e.g., France) (Harvey 1989, pp. 136–7). Although Fordism was not universal in its reach even at its height and problems abounded in its constituent parts (e.g., those of state capacity to contain/mollify losers and dissenters; the incomplete penetration of Fordist production methods, wage bargaining, and contract protections; and Third World dissatisfactions; see Harvey 1989, pp. 137–8), it held together under the umbrella of U.S. military and economic hegemony and produced high levels of worldwide economic expansion.

The Crisis of Fordism

The tendencies of capitalism toward "instability, crisis, and change" (Amin 1994, p. 7) eventually undermine the social arrangements that underpin an era of sustained capitalist accumulation. The first fundamental "crisis of capitalism" in this century, that of the 1930s, was primarily one of overproduction/underconsumption—the resolution of which involved state processes to regulate demand (via military spending and the welfare state, for instance). Welfare policies and the provision of consumer credit allowed consumption to continue during periods of recession and unemployment—features of the Fordist era largely absent in earlier times (Lipietz 1987, pp. 34–5).

In contrast, the "crisis of Fordism," which emerged in the 1970s, was not one of overproduction but of a profits squeeze. Declining rates of return on investment appeared across the advanced capitalist world, making the Fordist compromise between labor and capital more a liability than an asset.

> The Fordist operational modes engendered declining productivity gains while the technical composition of capital increased. This resulted in a fall of profitability that simultaneously diminished the capacity to accumulate; at the same time, accumulation led to less and less employment. As a consequence, the financing of the welfare state went into crisis. This, in turn, also decelerated the rhythm of accumulation. (Lipietz 1994, p. 30)

Declining rates of profit led firms to abandon cooperative relations with labor, instead cutting real wages, reducing employment, and minimizing tax obligations. The effects on demand and state finances were severe: Unemployed workers had less money to spend and made claims on welfare state programs at precisely the time when state revenues were squeezed by a drop in employment-based taxes and corporate receipts—a classic example of fiscal crisis (O'Connor 1973; Offe 1985).

The compromise, according to Lipietz, was "hit by crisis from all sides at once":

the lower profitability of the Fordist productive model, the internationalization of markets and production which compromised national regulation, workers turning against it because of alienation from work and because of the omnipotence of hierarchy and the state, citizens wanting more autonomy, and growing reservations about "administrative" [i.e., welfare state-imposed] solidarity. (Lipietz 1987, p. 12)

With more corporate competition conducted in an international market (rather than in largely oligopolistic national markets in which one's workers were also customers), high wages to a firm's workers constituted a drag on profits. Overseas markets were to be pursued in search of product buyers, hence resolving the "realization problem" without relying on a high-wage workforce at home. As noted by Jamie Peck and Adam Tickell,

> problems within the Fordist countries triggered the further internationalization of production. Keynesianism became discredited and monetarism increasingly influential. The internationalization of production and the growth of the export sector meant that wages were increasingly seen as a drag on economic competitiveness rather than a contributor to consumption. (Peck and Tickell 1994, p. 291)

After Fordism?

It is not clear what sort of associations will eventually replace Fordism as a stable context for capitalism (or whether in fact such will ever emerge). The current era exhibits features of the Fordist era (in some sectors of the advanced industrial countries and increasingly in hitherto peripheral areas of the world economy; see Chase-Dunn 1994, p. 100); simultaneously, it contains new and emerging patterns of economic, sociocultural, and political interaction. While the *ultimate* form of such new processes cannot be predicted with much confidence, the broad contours of these processes and relations are already well established. Variously described as post-fordist, late capitalism, globalization, or flexible accumulation, the emerging capitalist era differs in important respects from the Fordist accommodation.

Not all scholars would agree that these parameters are sufficiently well established (Amin 1994, pp. 1–2). Others, notably Michael Piore and Charles Sabel (1984, 1994), sketch a definitely more optimistic scenario of the future, envisioning the "flexible production" era as an emancipatory one built upon the return of craft-oriented production processes, greater labor-management teamwork, and the renaissance of regional economies.

Overall, I am persuaded that David Harvey's concept of flexible accumulation best describes the emerging, postfordist arrangements. Elements of the regime of accumulation that he describes can be seen in a variety of political and social contexts, and whatever mode of regulation eventually stabilizes around it will likely have most of the characteristics he describes (I will devote greater attention to sociocultural regulation matters in the next chapter).

To Harvey, flexible accumulation is typified by

> flexibility with respect to labour processes, labour markets, products, and patterns of consumption. It is marked by the emergence of entirely new sectors of production, new ways of providing financial services, new markets, and, above all, greatly intensified rates of commercial, technological, and organizational development . . . It has also entailed a new round of what I shall call "time-space compression" in the capitalist world—the time horizons of both private and public decision-making have shrunk, while satellite communication and declining transport costs have made it increasingly possible to spread those decisions immediately over an ever-wider and variegated space. (Harvey 1989, p. 147)

Flexible accumulation is marked by a far greater decentralization of production activities, tied together by increasingly sophisticated communications networks. This ever-greater corporate control over spatialization (Ross and Trachte 1990, pp. 7–8) has made possible a new system of labor utilization, one that has weakened labor unions, replaced full-time with part-time, subcontracted, and temporary labor, and increased the importance of home work, sweatshops, and other manifestations of the informal economy (Harvey 1989, pp. 147–55; Portes, Castells, and Benton 1989). This control over space-time built upon and further encouraged the deregulation of informational, financial, and media sectors throughout the industrialized world; as one perceptive analyst noted at the beginning of the 1980s, transnational finance and transnational information/media were becoming inextricably linked (Hamelink 1983), pulling both largely beyond the control of any given nation-state (see Schiller 1989, pp. 128–9; Harvey 1989, pp. 164–5).

Capitalism in the era of flexible accumulation differs from the Fordist regime in another critical respect. Mass-produced goods for largely undifferentiated masses of consumers seem less likely to dominate the future; a major role is emerging for customized, small-batch production for more fragmented markets. This has required speeded-up production times, just-in-time inventories, and greatly increased turnover time (Harvey 1989, p. 156).

However, as recognized at the dawn of the Fordist era in the 1920s (Ewen 1988; Fox and Lears 1983), speeded-up production is disastrous for capitalism unless matched by increased levels of consumption. In our time, problems of production have been replaced by the problem of consumption—how continually to increase its volume, expand the number of consumers, and extend it as the solution to an ever-wider range of human needs. Whereas during the Fordist era such a problem was largely limited to "societies of abundance" such as the United States, generating new avenues for consumption is now a global problem, among the central issues of the postfordist era, and is perhaps the primary nexus for cultural matters in international political economy.

From a liberal economic perspective, there seems to be nothing more bogus than the "problem of consumption"—that is, encouraging people to consume goods and services sufficient to keep the economy growing and reproducing. "Teaching people to consume," in a liberal mindset, is as inane as teaching fish to swim or dogs to bark. Human desires are limitless, infinite in their variety, with satiety a transitory state of repose.

Yet it is precisely in studying the "construction of consumption" as a constitutive (albeit generally underspecified) aspect of the globalization of the world economy that the centrality of "culture" emerges most forcefully. Reversing St. Paul's dictum ("anyone unwilling to work should not eat," 2 Thes 3:10), the postfordist economy dictates that if people will not eat (and drink and buy compact discs and travel abroad and purchase the latest in fashions, home appliances, and the like) in sufficient volume, then no one will work. John Kenneth Galbraith and others analyzed this emerging dynamic in the 1950s (Galbraith 1958); globalization has made the construction of particular consumption patterns a worldwide imperative, even (strangely enough) in very poor countries. "Consumerism" is reemerging as a major concentration in political economy, not simply as a moralistic condemnation of greed but also as a critically important feature of global capitalism. Whatever the final forms of the "mode of regulation" for capitalism after Fordism, it will doubtless include as major aspects those institutions, norms, and practices that relate to the construction of consumption (in appropriate degree and kind).

While regulation theory proves useful in analyzing many aspects of international political economy, it remains surprisingly underdeveloped in its treatment of the specifics of cultural institutions, relations, and phenomena; many regulation theorists seem content to discuss culture abstractly, in general terms (see Lee 1993, p. 89). Although other weaknesses in the approach have been noted as well (see Amin 1994, pp. 10–1; Chase-Dunn 1989), those concerned with the specifics of cultural phenomena are most important given the concerns of this book. I address the most important of these shortcomings regarding culture in the postfordist era in the next chapter. To understand the construction of consumption, the reciprocity of culture and capitalism in the global economy, and to see how all of this impacts hugely the survival of the gospel tradition, one must look beyond regulation theory. One must focus on some of the particulars of the global culture industries.

3

The Power of
Global Culture Industries

The globalization of capitalism's largest firms—in the automotive sector, in finance, consumer electronics, and the like—is familiar ground to most political economists. Until recently, however, the parallel (and often pace-setting) transnationalization in media, information, communications, and entertainment corporations has suffered from a relative lack of attention. No understanding of the present and likely future of the world economy—and how it affects the daily lives of billions of people—is complete without attention to these culture-oriented sectors.

For political economists and theologians alike, defining what sorts of enterprises constitute the "culture industries" is more difficult than it used to be when Max Horkheimer and Theodor Adorno applied the term primarily to mass communications media such as radio, cinema, and popular music (1944/1994 ed., pp. 120–67). On the one hand, these sorts of industries (which include television, advertising, book/magazine publishing, and the like) would still be of central importance. But the category today must also consider those industries that act as vectors, conveyors, or infra-structural requisites for cultural enterprises: included here must be telecommunications firms (such as Bell Atlantic, AT&T, MCI), computer interests (IBM, Apple, Microsoft), and infomatics and data-processing/generating firms (such as TRW, Equifax, market research firms). Finally, one must account for the role of cultural products as *inputs* into the production of myriad other commercial products: everything from trademarks and brands, packaging and marketing strategies, to product design and positioning. Indeed, as will be illustrated herein, the impact of culture industries in the flexible accumulation stage of capitalism ranges far beyond the profit/loss statements of TCI, Disney, CBS, MGM, or other culture industries (defined in the narrow, traditional sense).

There now exists a literature on trends in the global culture industries: for example, on television (Quester 1990; Hilliard and Keith 1996; Sinclair, Jacka, and Cunningham 1996); advertising (Mattelart 1991); music (Malm and Wallis 1992); in publishing and entertainment media (Barnet and Cavanagh 1994); in European media (Tunstall and Palmer 1991); and in news (Reeves 1993). Across sectors, several trends seem common:

1. National variations with regard to major culture industries—especially, but not only, television and radio—are diminishing. Public service broadcast systems are being privatized in whole or in part, monopoly and quasi-monopoly market structures are being replaced by competition driven by commercial, for-profit media properties. Deregulation in broadcasting is a global trend, and advertising is becoming a dominant, near-universal media funding base, even in countries where ad-supported broadcasting had been prohibited or severely circumscribed (Tunstall and Palmer 1991; Hilliard and Keith 1996). Although the pace of such change is uneven, there are few if any exceptions to the *direction* of such change (instances of nationalization or decommodification of culture industries are hard to find since the early to mid-1970s). Large areas of public cultural expression and consumption are now dominated by large, for-profit corporations whose scope of operations are increasingly transnational.

2. Divisions within culture industries are softening somewhat due to the integration of industries and overlapping technologies (digital processes, for example) and to corporate strategies that gather a range of culture producers (film production, music company, home video, television interests, marketing division, etc.) under one roof as part of a "synergistic" corporate strategy.

3. Culture industries are seen as increasingly valuable to other sorts of corporations (manufacturers, financial houses), who acquire/divest the former with a steady level of enthusiasm. One review of corporate mergers/acquisitions of culture industries (broadly defined to include telecoms, software firms, and the like) found 160 deals in 1993, worth more than $75 billion (Hughes 1994).

The business and academic press has chronicled the rise of giant global firms in the culture industries. Time-Warner, the largest media conglomerate in the world, originated in a 1980s-era merger that created a firm generating total sales of $8.9 billion by 1989 (Smith 1991, p. 24). Its publishing-related holdings alone include diverse properties such as *Enter-*

tainment Weekly, Little, Brown and Co., Warner Books, Book-of-the-Month Club, Children's Book-of-the-Month Club, Warner Publishing Services (which distributes more than 40 magazines and book titles for 90 other publishers), and more than 60 regular comic books (including *Superman, Batman, Wonder Woman,* and the rest of the D.C. Comics roster). It also holds a diverse portfolio of magazine, television, music, and film companies (Wasko 1994, pp. 49–51).

Time-Warner is one of the handful of companies that comprises what commentator Tom Frank describes as the "Culture Trust"—those firms "whose assorted vice-presidents now supervise almost every aspect of American [and increasingly, worldwide] public expression" (Frank 1995, p. 6).

Another member of that select group, the Disney Group, once boasted that on an August weekend in 1990, 30 percent of all movie theaters in the United States and Canada were screening a feature produced by one of Disney's production companies (Wasko 1994, p. 53). Disney is among the most effective practitioners of cross-promotion, utilizing the various Disney subsidiaries to encourage consumption of one another's products and images. As Ron Grover observes:

> By late 1988, the Disney channel was . . . achieving [CEO Michael] Eisner's goal of cross-promotion for other company ventures. Kids watching Winnie the Pooh or Mickey Mouse cartoons became a target market for Disney toys. Showing episodes of *The Mickey Mouse Club,* which had been filmed at the Disney-MGM Studio Theme Park, enticed 14-year-olds into pressuring their parents to take them to Orlando. When *Who Framed Roger Rabbit* was aired on the channel, specials on EPCOT Center were also run, along with anniversary shows celebrating the parks. (Grover 1991, pp. 198, 190; quoted in Wasko 1994, p. 54)

Disney's cross-promotional strategies will likely intensify in the wake of its $19 billion acquisition of the ABC television network in 1995.

Such diversification is the norm not only for major United States cultural conglomerates, but also for those such as Sony, Bertelsman, Berlusconi, and Rupert Murdoch's News Corporation. This type of broad-based positioning emerges from the desire of firms to sustain profit margins endangered by deregulation and from the need to maintain a healthy image in world financial markets, from which they raise much of their capital (Smith 1991, pp. 9–10, 26–8, 30–4, 37). As Anthony Smith notes:

Publishers want to be in a position to exploit a work of talent across the whole media landscape; they have come to fear the consequences of being excluded from an audience if they do not have a finger in every kind of media pie. Furthermore, it is becoming easier in technological terms to become involved in a wider range of media. Transnational media empires are thus coming into being to exploit new opportunities and as a protection against possible losses of opportunity. (Smith 1991, p. 15)

Culture industries figure prominently in national-level economic analysis; cultural exports from the United States in 1989 accounted for an $8 billion trade surplus, trailing only the aerospace and agribusiness sectors as contributors to U.S. export strength (Barnet and Cavanagh 1994, p. 25). Disputes over whether national culture industries, including cinema and television, should be deregulated as part of the GATT process were among the most bitter disputes of the Uruguay Round concluded in 1994. And the leaders of the G-7 countries have made common policies on telecommunications and cultural products (emphasizing deregulation, intellectual property rights, and competition) a major priority in shaping the future of the world economy (Nash 1995, p. C-1).

But while many of the products of global culture industries are heavily influenced by American production values and styles, they are not exclusively U.S. in ownership. As two observers note:

It is now obvious that you do not have to be American to sell American culture. Japanese corporations have bought major Hollywood studios and are looking for more. Only three of America's largest studios are still U.S. companies. Six global corporations dominate the popular music industry, not only in the United States but across the world . . . only one of the six, Warner, is still a U.S. company. (Barnet and Cavanagh 1994, p. 26)

What had once been a near-monopoly for certain U.S.-based entertainment and culture industries worldwide now more closely resembles a multinational oligopoly in which the players include firms based in Japan and Europe. These changes have not led to greater decentralization or broader ownership of cultural industries; on the contrary, as Smith concludes, "the really powerful outlets for creative work in print and the moving images [among other industries] seem all to be slipping into the capacious hands of a group of giant industrial companies" (1991, p. 3). Beneath these global firms, a handful of smaller regional/linguistic oligopolists engage in a delicate dance of competition and cooperation with the giant firms (Sinclair, Jacka, and Cunningham 1996, pp. 11–4).

The global culture industries, as significant as they are in their own right, take on added significance when one situates them in the larger context of flexible accumulation (or "postfordist") capitalism. The activities of this sector increasingly frame the opportunities, limitations, and openings for other firms as globalization proceeds apace. These industries are "the economic dynamos of the new age," according to one observer:

> the economically crucial tools by which the public is informed of the latest offerings, enchanted by packaged bliss, instructed in the arcane pleasures of the new, taught to be good citizens, and brought warmly into the consuming fold. Every leader of business now knows that the nation's health is measured not by production of cars or corn but by the strength of its culture industry. (Frank 1995, pp. 5–6)

As anthropological insights continue to enrich the study of political economy, the inextricably "cultural" importance of goods, services, and consumption has received increased attention in the business and scholarly literature (e.g., Belk, Wallendorf, and Sherry 1989; Lee 1993). One insight from this literature concerns the processes by which various meanings, identities, and representations are attached to commodities over time. Although such processes are not automatic or mechanical, neither are they random; some institutions and actors have disproportionate influence in delimiting or encouraging the range of meanings and associations ascribed to certain commodities or consumption processes.

Here is another reason why the culture industries are central to understanding postfordist capitalism: More than any other set of social institutions, these industries collectively influence how people relate to the processes and products of economic activity. Movies, television, popular music, advertising—these are the vectors and initiators for ideas regarding the valued, the innovative, the normal, the erotic, and the repulsive. As will be seen subsequently, this makes the workings of culture industries an important influence on matters of human subjectivity and agency—which have always been important in understanding the workings of capitalism in any given era.

Advertising/Marketing as a
Global Culture Industry

Among the traditional culture industries, I argue that advertising and marketing hold places of central importance. I am aware that advertising and marketing are often considered separately in the business literature, but I am more impressed—for present purposes, anyway—by their similarities. To make my claim even stronger, I argue that the advertising/ marketing sector is crucial for the ongoing reproduction of postfordist capitalism as a transnational phenomenon.

Such is not to say that all culture industries are identical, nor that the visible trends and structures of the advertising/marketing sector are exactly the same as those in cinema, television, infomatics, and the like. But, as I hope to demonstrate, the trends I identified earlier in this chapter (global moves toward commercialization, interpenetration of industries, and the integration of culture industries in large corporate conglomerates) point to the penetration of advertising/marketing into most other realms of cultural production.

In the American (and now global) context, as noted by critic Herbert Schiller,

> for advertising to fulfill its systemically crucial role—getting the national output of goods and services into the hands and homes of buyers, and reaffirming daily, if not hourly, that consumption is the definition of democracy—it must have full access to the nation's message-making and message-transmitting apparatus. Over time this means the transformation of the press, radio, television cable, and every such subsequent technology into instruments of marketing.
>
> This is done with single-minded devotion. It has succeeded so well that the nation's image- and message-making machinery has been almost fully directed to salesmanship. The press is dependent on advertising for approximately three-quarters of its income. Commercial radio and television are totally reliant on advertising revenues, and the public channels, too, are increasingly dependent on this source of support . . . What the record reveals is an almost total takeover of the domestic informational system for the purposes of selling goods and services. (Schiller 1994, p. 33)

As I see it, scrutiny of the advertising/marketing segment of the global culture industries acts as a lens through which one can apprehend the rest of the culture industries and their place in postfordist capitalism. To talk seriously about advertising/marketing is necessarily to talk seriously about the rest of the culture industries and about the relationship between "political economy" and "culture." The importance of these developments to those interested in the preconditions for the practice of Christian discipleship will be explored in the next two chapters.

The Global Discourse of
Marketing and Advertising

Among the transnational culture industries, those associated with advertising (and marketing, the more general field) hold a place of central importance. The activity of this sector increasingly frames the opportunities, limitations, and openings for other firms as globalization proceeds apace. The academic and professional literature attests to the centrality that advertising and promotion play in transnational corporate aspirations and strategies; a critical examination of this literature reveals several considerations key to understanding the role of advertising and marketing in the globalizing political economy. Certainly, as an industry advertising worldwide has experienced phenomenal growth and concentration in the past twenty years. The globalization affecting other culture industries has impacted advertising in a similar fashion: A handful of firms now dominate the world advertising industry. British firms in particular have benefited from the globalization trend; at one point, six of the world's twenty largest firms and the two largest worldwide (WPP and Saatchi & Saatchi) were of British origin. WPP acquired the fifth-largest agency, the American firm J. Walter Thompson, in 1987, and later added the world's foremost market research firm (Market Research Bureau), and a world leader in direct marketing (Ogilvy and Mather) (Mattelart 1991, pp. 1–2, 6, 23).

Mergers and acquisitions were not the only means of concentrating global advertising strength; several critical joint ventures, established in the 1980s, added to the reach and diversity of global agency networks. Most important was the joint venture that created HDM in 1987; this entity, created by the two largest American and Japanese firms and the foremost French agency, brought together 95 offices in 24 countries (Mattelart 1991, pp. 14–5). And while large global advertising firms have increased their share of expanding world advertising revenues (and absorbing or integrating smaller, locally attuned firms), the range of services provided by these agencies is also expanding. The first global agency, Saatchi & Saatchi, provided the model for many:

> They aimed to transform the advertising agency, to become an operational think-tank capable of intervening in every segment of what Saatchis, in its annual reports, calls the "business culture," and to compete openly on their own terrain with the leading consultants, market research companies, and accountants. (Mattelart 1991, p. 10)

In what global firms tout as "integrated communications" services, non-advertising activities are providing an increasing proportion of agency revenues. J. Walter Thompson, for example, derives nearly half its revenue from research, public relations, design, sales promotion, and video communication; Ogilvy and Mather, similarly, derives nearly 40 percent of its revenue from direct marketing, public relations, and research (Mattelart 1991, p. 24). These trends flow into the rise of "micromarketing" in advanced capitalist countries, as niche marketing and fragmented audiences replace the once-dominant, relatively homogeneous mass market.

Given the problems associated with the density of commercial messages (called "clutter") in advanced capitalist countries, global agencies eagerly await further expansion of the world market into less advertising-drenched cultures. Of the $240 billion spent worldwide on advertising and marketing in 1989, half went into the North American market, 28 percent toward Europe, 19 percent into Asia and the Pacific (Japan is the world's second-largest ad market behind the United States), and only 2 percent to Latin America and 1 percent into Africa and the Middle East (Mattelart 1991, pp. 36–7). These latter markets are considered underserved and domains of future expansion. Although barriers to penetration and adaptation to local markets will endure into the future, it seems likely that the future belongs to global rather than national or subnational advertising corporations; the regionalization of world markets (post–1992 Europe and Eastern Europe, the North American and East Asian trade enclaves) will likely accelerate these trends (see for example Cook 1992, p. 7).

On the Need for a "Postmodern" Appraisal of Advertising

When assessing global culture industries, attention to these sorts of institutional features—market structure, concentration, integration across sec-

tors—must be considered. To more fully understand the culture industries, however, one must situate these institutional features in wider political, economic, and cultural contexts. Along with some other commentators (e.g., Harvey 1989), I argue that a postmodern social/cultural
environment corresponds to the economic and political changes represented by the contemporary phase of capitalism. Although a full description of postmodern culture is beyond the scope of this chapter, its central
relevant characteristics suggest the following:

- The cultural environment of contemporary capitalism is unlike any
  that has ever existed. Exposure to mediated messages and experiences is more voluminous, more continuous, and more pervasive
  than ever before (see Schiller 1989; Thompson 1990). Advertising
  messages in particular are ubiquitous, round-the-clock back-
  grounds to our daily lives—they are in all environments, from gro-
  cery stores and streets to hospitals, bedrooms, and churches. The
  output of other culture industries—movies, television, music
  videos, recorded music, and the like—adds further to the unprecedented commercial and symbolic saturation of life in contemporary
  capitalism. One observer estimates that persons in the United
  States are exposed to 16,000 commercial messages, symbols, and
  reminders every day (Savan 1994, p. 1).
- The sheer volume, diversity, and transitoriness of cultural production have largely sundered ties between symbols and their referents, a phenomenon known as fragmentation (Jameson 1991, pp.
  26–7; Firat 1991, p. 71). Symbols can no longer be assumed to
  have a constant, universally understood relationship to some independent, "real" referent; rather, symbols in the commercial culture
  are constantly recombined, reshuffled, and replaced with an eye
  toward conveying novel "meanings" to various products and consumption opportunities (Firat 1991). "Meaning," in such a world,
  is constructed from a goulash of symbols, narratives, and prior
  "meanings" in play in the cultural environment; any given symbol
  is likely to have "polyvalent meaning," a multitude of different
  meanings depending on how it is appropriated by different sub-
  groups within an audience. These detached symbols and clusters
  of meaning are aligned, paired, or similarly "transferred" to consumption opportunities by marketers and others who must generate demand adequate for profitability and the healthy functioning
  of the economy.

- The social ideals of the postmodern era differ in important ways from those of the previous one. When capital accumulation and savings were needed for the health of the capitalist system, values related to the Protestant ethic were lionized—those of thrift, sobriety, austerity, and dedication to work. As already noted, in the postmodern era problems of productive capacity have been largely overcome in the advanced capitalist countries, only to be replaced by those of consumptive capacity. Capitalism now needs high, even profligate, levels of consumer spending to function smoothly; were people to cease consuming once their basic needs were met, the system would collapse. So, just as austerity-based values were rewarded when production-based problems were primary, now those values must be replaced by others better suited to solving consumption-based problems. The Protestant ethic is dysfunctional in the consumption-driven postmodern era (except in the workplace, where hard work for the boss remains central); hedonism, indulgence, short-term pleasure now must have pride of place, at least when off the job. As Harvey notes, the more fluid nature of capital leads to emphases culturally on "the new, the fleeting, the ephemeral, the fugitive, and the contingent" in modern life. However, he adds that, as suggested earlier by Georg Simmel, such fragmented and insecure times also lead to "a heightened emphasis upon the authority of basic institutions—the family, religion, the state. And there is abundant evidence of a revival of such institutions and the values they represent throughout the Western world since about 1970" (Harvey 1989, p. 171).

But such "traditional" institutions are not left unchanged by current developments. To a large but varying extent, they have themselves already been radically reshaped by these new economic processes—hence the seeming paradox of the 1980s of postmodern hedonism simultaneous with a "return to traditional values."

The nature of advertising appeals has changed dramatically since the industry's earliest days. Leiss, Kline, and Jhally (1990) are among those who have documented the shift in message appeals from utilitarian, product-focused ads toward the buyer-centered, image-related approaches that dominate contemporary advertising. Contemporary advertising creations "generally do not present logical arguments and claims for their products. Instead, they seek to associate their product with evocative images and themes" (Strate 1991, p. 113). Advertising discourse and practice in postmodern culture, according to critics and practitioners alike, are infused with myth, narrative, symbolism, and the raw materials of nonmarket cultural codes, traditions, and meanings. One marketer talks of creating an emotional bond between consumers and a product brand, about "creating mythologies about their brands by humanizing them and giving them distinct personalities and cultural sensibilities" (*Marketing News*, Feb. 17, 1992, p. 19).

In such a context—a media-saturated environment with ceaseless, meaning-laden market appeals—a revised epistemological standpoint is required for analysis and action. In earlier times, when the commercialization of everyday life was less thorough, media studies focused on the effects of individual messages, ads, or programs (see Verbeke 1992, p. 1; Harvey 1989, p. 287; Mattelart 1991, p. 213). In the contemporary situation, in which the flow (unceasing, reinforcing, in multiple media) of commercial, mediated symbols is the dominant reality, concentrating on single messages or ads seems unjustifiably reductionist. Whatever effects derive from commercial culture, such can only be effects of the total flow—and the significance of any single item in that flow can be ascertained only in relation to other items in that flow. In place of a linear, behaviorist epistemology ("Does commercial A produce the expected behavior/attitude change?"), one must necessarily substitute a more interpretive, subjective methodology.

Power, Knowledge, and Advertising/Marketing

The preferred public image that the advertising industry offers worldwide is one of service—to consumers (by providing needed information on products and prices), to firms (by providing access to consumers), and to society (by promoting freedom of choice and individual autonomy, the requisites of a free society). It is not an industry, in this view, that exercises power over anyone anywhere—this world is one of rational, informed, and autonomous consumers, one in which consumer sovereignty reigns over the weak, imprecise, and reactive institutions of marketing. Far from being an institution exercising power, advertising is a bulwark of free enterprise and democracy, defending against bureaucrats, top-down planners, and other enemies of freedom. Because of this, advertising is an "early target for attack" aimed at economic freedom and democratic governance (Vale 1992, p. 4).

Much of the advertising/marketing literature presents a public face of respect for consumer rationality, only to act and speak from radically different assumptions in more technical, in-house environments. One vivid example of such bifurcation shines in a popular book by Richard Ott, a marketing consultant (1992). He begins with the obligatory bow to the consumer as king and declares the impossibility of manipulating consumers (1992, pp. vii–ix). The next 200-plus pages combine an appreciation for sophisticated psychographic research with systematic advice on how to "create demand" by targeting subconscious, nonrational, and emotion-laden psychological processes. This nontechnical book, at once a piece of self-promotion and popularization of widely shared ideas and practices, testifies to a false deference paid to consumer rationality and independence by the advertising/marketing industry.

In contrast, the view I advance is that marketing and advertising in a postmodern context represent techniques of power in the contemporary world—that is, a web of observation, surveillance, and attempts at behavior modification that stretches from the global culture industries down to the isolated consumer/individual. Marketing and advertising construct a discourse and relationality of power—derived from knowledge about, and strategies targeted at, individuals who exist in an asymmetrical relation with the firms and conglomerates that drive the global consumption machine. It is a new phenomenon in the capitalist world economy—a macro-micro, transnational link with individuals around the world, relatively unmediated by sovereign states. The link intends to affect the attitudes, behaviors, ideologies, and nonconscious dispositions of its objects.

This sense of power derives from the later work of Michel Foucault (1979, 1980). In his many inquiries into the histories of important institutional bases of modernity—prisons, hospitals, schools, and the like—Foucault describes how the exercise of power has shifted over time. While the exercise of power once produced exemplars of coercive, often incredibly cruel, force (to compensate for irregularity or inefficiency in application), modern institutions gradually adopted power strategies that were less overtly coercive, more concerned with molding behaviors and attitudes, and more concerned with achieving regularity, ongoing observation, and information useful in improving methods of socialization and further information gathering (see in general Foucault 1979, 1980; also Hoy 1986, pp. 12–3; Smart 1986, p. 161).

Hence, although prisons, schools, and the like are usually less overtly oppressive than in the past, their efficiency in constructing categories of social significance—the criminal, the educated, and the ignorant—has increased. Further, the behavior- and attitude-shaping functions of these institutions are enhanced by practices of social observation, research, and surveillance directed toward target populations—which generate new knowledge these institutions utilize in further improving their efforts. It is in this sense that power functions in a "positive" fashion, according to Foucault—not just in prohibiting, deterring, or threatening ("negative" power), but in generating new knowledge, new behaviors, new norms and expectations, and new social conceptions of truth (e.g., Foucault 1980, pp. 93, 107, 139–40).

Further, these contemporary networks of power do not derive solely from state or sovereign power, nor are they reducible to the domination of one class over another. In their origins and maintenance, they are largely without a primary or central subject—not the sovereign nor the ruling class, not a predetermined strategy to generate social conformity. Rather, these institutionalized webs of power and knowledge are assemblies of strategies developed piecemeal via localized trial and error, which then are diffused, adopted, and articulated as they demonstrate benefits (originally foreseen or not) or effectiveness. Given the importance of state and corporate actors in these processes, however, I am not persuaded by Foucault's argument for the "acephalic" quality of power-knowledge in the areas under discussion here.

The world of contemporary marketing and advertising displays many fundamentals that are best understood in these terms. To see how it represents a power-laden phenomenon (rather than a more benign manifestation of corporate free speech, as a more liberal view would suggest), one ought to consider several important aspects of postmodern advertising.

The major shift in twentieth-century advertising theory and practice, from product-centered to consumer-centered, increased the role of information in advertising. Knowledge about consumers became a prized commodity; it came to affect not only all aspects of sales and marketing but eventually nearly all other aspects of corporate strategy.

Advanced industrial societies are so thoroughly scrutinized by commercial interests—which gather and utilize information on births, deaths, ages, occupations, weddings, credit histories, addresses, reading habits, sexual behaviors, educational levels, illnesses, hobbies, fears, fantasies, childrearing practices, cultural heroes, religious values, pet ownership, and countless other phenomena—that it is easy to forget how truly radical, asymmetrical, and constitutive of our social environment are such information-gathering and information-utilizing practices. Traditional demographic categories have long been an important aspect of such information collection and observation; in the contemporary, postmodern context, new types of knowledge about consumers are critical. Many of these new sorts of knowledge focus on subconscious or nonrational phenomena; giving the lie to notions of consumer sovereignty and rationality, various programs of psychographic research continue searching for emotional, precognitive, and value-based "triggers" that can be grasped in efforts to generate consumption-oriented behaviors (see Piirto 1991 for a business-oriented history of psychographic research; see also Kamakure and Novak 1992 and Goerne 1992 for examples). Those words, concepts, pictures, sounds, and other components that "resonate" favorably among various segments of mass markets (determined by extensive advance testing and research) become the stuff of modern ad appeals (e.g., Piirto 1991, pp. 90–1). Sophisticated psychological testing continues to search for knowledge about people unknown to the individuals themselves and for reliable advertising strategies capable of translating that knowledge into corporate-desired behaviors or attitudes (Piirto 1991, p. 14, pp. 126–8; Goerne 1992, p. H-32). In this regard, according to Oscar Gandy, Jr. (1993, p. 68), "every day, thousands of U.S. consumers participate in [market and psychological] experiments without the benefit of having any informed consent forms." While largely developed in the United States, such research approaches are increasingly utilized on a global scale (Piirto 1991, pp. 142–66; *Marketing News*, Aug. 26, 1987; Marriott 1986).

Marketing—as an institution generating powerful knowledge—operates increasingly as a fully articulated system, constantly integrating feedback (performance and outcome data, unanticipated effects, the impact and experiences of other marketers) into new strategies and research. Information about potential customers is generated from seemingly limitless sources—from credit card transactions to hidden cameras in supermarkets used to observe consumer responses to various display, position, price, and other strategies. The immense knowledge-generating potential of barcoded data gathering systems ("scanner" technology in multiple forms) is only now becoming apparent and is becoming a pervasive feature of advanced industrial societies.

According to Oscar Gandy:

> The importance of the development of scanner technology cannot be overstated. Scanning from point-of-purchase terminals, such as the checkout counter in the supermarket, provides data at high speed and in real time about the status of the market as well as the responsiveness of consumers to variations in price and representation . . . But the scanning technology also

provides the organization with the option of gathering this information at the level of purchases by identified individuals. Special mailings or other distributions of promotional materials to persons whose identities are scanned at the time they pay for their purchases facilitates the linkage between inventory control and marketing central to the emerging just-in-time approach to manufacturing, which links production to consumption. (Gandy 1993, p. 66)

To repeat, marketing/advertising power, in this view, does not operate in a "hypodermic" fashion, implanting ideas and desires into the minds of countless passive individuals. Nor does it assume that people are stupid, easily duped, or incapable of choice. Its dynamic is more closely akin to a seduction than an assault. It involves actor A knowing things about B that B doesn't realize A knows. It is like playing poker against someone who has already seen your hand, unbeknownst to you, in a blurred mirror. In such a context, the actor under surveillance chooses, she is acting freely, but she does so in a context constructed to advance the priorities of others. So long as the asymmetry in information persists, and so long as the player under surveillance is unaware of the degree of contextual manipulation and structuring, the one-sided interaction can continue indefinitely. And the fact that the surveillance is imperfect (it cannot accurately connect with resonant symbols, etc., every time) only adds to the illusion of an interaction among free, equal parties, insofar as not all advertising "works"; just as peeking at another's poker hand via a blurred mirror provides a less-than-perfect picture of another's hand.

Again, to reiterate Foucault's insight, no single individual or group is "directing" this power complex, and no class stands "above" it looking down on another; there is no easily isolated agency to investigate. Indeed, that no one escapes it—not even the marketers themselves—makes it appear benign, natural, and/or power-neutral. Nevertheless, the importance of this dense web of behaviors, observations, messages, and sanctions—conforming to the needs and aspirations of profit-driven corporations—should not be minimized. It both isolates people—constructing a particular type of consumerist "individuality"—and subordinates them into a "totalizing unity," as do other power/knowledge complexes (Rabinow 1984, p. 22). Such is explicit in the coming era of "global communication" described by the president of Dentsu, Japan's largest ad agency: "It is a form of communication that transcends national boundaries and language and reaches to the hearts and minds of people. Global communication must speak personally to every individual; at the same time its message must be universal" (quoted in Mattelart 1991, pp. 57–8). The impact of advertising/marketing practices in shaping social and cultural values is admitted by actors inside and outside the marketing world (for example, see Verbeke 1992, p. 6, on marketing as an "environment shaping" process; see also Tse, Belk, and Zhou 1989, pp. 457–8).

In the more fully developed consumer cultures, advertising strives to perpetuate processes it helped initiate—especially the ongoing creation and re-creation of personal styles, identities, lifestyles, and social networks via fluid and transitory consumption packages. "Associative advertising" is one technique (summarized by Waide 1987, pp. 73–4) common in consumer cultures. It involves, among other things, the following characteristics:

- Advertising strategies that identify a "deep-seated nonmarket good for which people in the target market feel a strong desire." Such a good is one which cannot by definition be bought and sold in markets (for example friendship, acceptance, and esteem). In most cases the marketed product "bears only the most tenuous (if any) relation to the nonmarket good with which it is associated in the advertising campaign. For example, soft drinks cannot give one friends, sex, or excitement."
- "If possible, the desire for the nonmarket good is intensified by calling into question one's acceptability." Advertising associates the product with a nonmarket value it cannot possibly satisfy, while stimulating feelings of personal inadequacy and anxiety.
- The satisfaction of the nonmarket value exploited by associative advertising is partial at best and is usually due to advertising's cultural impact.

For example, mouthwash has little prolonged effect on stinking breath, but it helps to reduce the intense anxieties reinforced by mouthwash commercials on television because we at least feel that we are doing the proper thing. In the most effective cases of associative advertising, people begin to talk like ad copy. We begin to sneer at those who own the wrong things. We all become enforcers for the advertisers. In general, if the advertising images are effective enough and reach enough people, even preposterous marketing claims can become at least partially self-fulfilling. (Waide 1987, pp. 73–4)

The possible combinations of images and products in a postmodern culture are nearly limitless—associations can change over time to exploit perceived opportunities, and marketers can appropriate new codes devel-oped within subcultures (e.g., punk fashions). With no strong ties be-tween images and referents (a phenomenon known as fragmentation; see Jameson 1991, pp. 26–7; Furat 1991, p. 71) and with constant demands to accelerate product turnover and purchasing, advertising has come to as-sume "a much greater importance in the growth dynamics of capitalism" (Harvey 1989, p. 287).

Exporting the Power Matrix

From cars to cosmetics to Pepsi-Cola, many global conglomerates increas-ingly envision the sources of their future growth and profits in the predom-inantly poor regions of the world system. Auto executives contemplating hundreds of millions of potential Chinese drivers are "drooling" with antic-ipation, according to *Business Week* ("New worlds to conquer," 1994, p. 50). India's gross domestic product, by some estimates, will surpass that of France, Italy, and Great Britain in the next few decades (Spielvogel 1991, p. 89). Realizing the full profit potential of these Third World regions re-quires the deployment of the full complement of advertising/marketing techniques utilized so successfully in advanced industrial countries.

For the consumption-constructing techniques to be exported from their regions of origin to the hoped-for "growth regions" of future demand, sev-eral prerequisites must be met. These involve the construction of support-ive institutional, policy, and technical networks, upon which the advertis-ing/marketing processes discussed earlier can then expand.

The consumption-constructing techniques to which I refer should not be equated with simple mass advertising, which has had a worldwide spread (at least in major urban areas) for decades. The technical package at issue here is more integrated (with tighter, recursive feedback loops joining present consumer activity, marketing interventions, and future consumer activity) and multilayered than simple mass-advertising campaigns.

While the following requisites need not be complete before firms can exploit consumption-constructing tools (indeed, the expansion of firms utilizing such tools can accelerate the development of such requisites), their full exploitation requires changes involving

- the deregulation of mass media, including loosening of restrictions on advertising, the emergence of commercial media, and a greater reliance on market mechanisms over public administrative proce-dures;

- the construction of the technical infrastructure that enables firms to penetrate widely into social, family, marketplace, and individual space, including, but not limited to, telecommunications, television, radio, postal services, and computer/computer support services;
- the establishment of global advertising/marketing and research firms capable of joining sophisticated technical expertise with knowledge of local cultures, histories, and customs.

The combined pressures from multilateral agencies, such as the IMF and World Bank, global producers, media and advertising conglomerates, and aggressive market-oriented states (e.g., the U.S. under Reagan, the U.K. during the Thatcher years) have effected substantial changes worldwide in the regulatory environments of media firms and advertisers. This is true whether one speaks of "public-interest" broadcast systems, increased commercial broadcast presence worldwide, loosened restrictions on advertising practices, or more concentrated ownership patterns involving media firms.

In like fashion, many of the aforementioned actors have been instrumental in constructing the physical/technical infrastructures necessary for a more thoroughly postmodern mediated environment to exist in poor countries. In this, something resembling a mutually reinforcing process has taken shape. World Bank loans for construction of telecommunications networks (public and private) have been important in many countries (see Hills 1994, p. 185); removal of limits on foreign direct investment (a demand pushed by the IMF, World Bank, international banks, and Northern governments) has made possible the entry of global telecoms, media, and information-processing firms into poor countries as privatization and deregulation proceed.

The uneven penetration of such telecommunications and information-processing industries in poor countries testifies to the degree of prior insertion by consumer electronics, media, and related firms in these regions. Africa, the Middle East, and much of Asia show lower levels of television ownership, for example, than does Latin America. Although most Latin American countries have high TV ownership figures (in one compilation for major countries, penetration figures ranged from a low of 67 percent in Peru to 98 percent in Uruguay, 97 percent in Argentina, and 90 percent in Chile), the virtual absence of cable and satellite usage invites expansion in these latter areas in the future (*Intermedia*, 1993, p. 14).

Concerning the third requisite, although the pace of global mergers and acquisitions involving media, marketing, and advertising firms has slowed since the fever years of the mid-1980s, the process continues nonetheless. Northern-based media giants continue to expand, occasionally in partnership with regional or language-based oligopolies. Although the most recent recession hit hard some pioneering global advertising firms such as Saatchi & Saatchi, global advertising/marketing firms continue to expand their operations worldwide, both by acquiring small local firms and by taking on independent locals as junior partners (Mattelart 1991, pp. 56–7). The advertising industry continues to expand training and educational programs in emerging markets to ensure its supply of local creative and managerial personnel (on potential talent shortfalls and the need for increased training by transnational ad agencies, see Shao and Hill 1992). Advertising/marketing firms will continue to expand and enlarge if they expect to serve their major clients, nearly all of whom are "globalizing" in search of markets and profits.

If any piece in the puzzle remains inadequate, it is that of market research in its many varieties. In part, this lag derives from the absence, until recently, of the other elements discussed previously. In any event, information-producing firms and activities are expanding rapidly throughout poor regions of the world; this drag on the consumer-constructing package will diminish in the foreseeable future, albeit not at a uniform pace.

For example, A.C. Nielsen, the powerful U.S. market research firm, recently acquired the largest supplier of consumer research data in Asia. This firm, Survey Research Group (SRG), is a Hong Kong–based entity with operations in Australia, Canada, China, Indonesia, Japan, Korea, Singapore, Malaysia, New Zealand, the Philippines, Taiwan, Thailand, Vietnam, and the United States. It has been described by one Nielsen executive as "the 800-pound gorilla of market research in Asia," the acquisition of which was seen as "very important for our customers around the world" (Yates 1994, p. 1). Other market-research firms boast an active presence in Central and South America, Africa, India, and other non-European regions (*American Demographics*, 1994, p. 38).

Conspicuously absent from this list of prerequisites is any requirement concerning minimal levels of economic growth, distribution of purchasing power, or broad-based prosperity. Although there are legitimate reasons to suppose that industries selling products designed initially for a Northern middle-class market will prefer to see purchasing power in poor countries skewed in the direction of greater inequality (Evans 1979), not all globalizing sellers fit this profile. It seems more likely to apply to sellers of automobiles than soft drinks, for example; additionally, increasingly important "new markets" display highly divergent profiles regarding income and wealth inequality (although for most, growing inequality is the trend, as it is in most Northern countries). This latter effect, stemming from the growing role of market forces worldwide, is polarizing wealth and income figures between and within countries. In any event, while the export of consumer-producing techniques may *affect* distribution of social product, there does not appear to be any prior distributional profile necessary for the export of such techniques. The only exception seems to be some minimal level of disposable cash income, although some market professionals stress sales opportunities to elites in even the most destitute regions of Africa (Cutler 1989, p. 16).

China: The Export Package Arrives

The emergence of the People's Republic of China from a largely self-sufficient and semi-autarchic era into the global capitalist economy provides a case study-in-motion of how the consumption-export package works. Indeed, one prominent group of marketing researchers describe the process as an "unprecedented and bold experiment" that seeks to inculcate a consumerist ethic in China (Belk and Zhou 1986, pp. 478–9). They are concerned with "how a society learns to consume" and study China as an example of "how societies learn to desire an escalating agenda of contemporary consumption objects" (Tse, Belk, and Zhou 1989, p. 457).

One important piece in this puzzle concerns the rapid rise, and basically open-ended future, of Western-owned satellite television broadcasting. Two rivals—STAR TV, owned by Rupert Murdoch, and TVB, a consortium joining the world's largest producer of Chinese-language programming with CNN, ESPN, HBO, and the Australian AUSTV—are expanding the reach of commercial television throughout Asia. Western-style regional and local advertising will support these efforts, and veteran Western executives have assumed important positions in both organizations, in part, to smooth the recruiting of advertisers (e.g., "Television's Final Frontier," *Economist,* July 31, 1993, p. 57).

With its financial base and programming supply increasingly secure, satellite firms such as STAR TV and TVB can concentrate on increasing the availability of satellite dishes and cable systems. In response to the availability of this satellite-borne programming, numerous local firms are providing both individual home-reception dishes (now only 18 inches in diameter, thanks to technical advances) and commercial cable systems in

China. Some estimates suggest that, despite formal (but infrequently enforced) restrictions on ownership, more than 500,000 dishes were sold in China in 1992 alone to complement 2,000 cable systems (some estimates on reach and audience are far higher; see "STAR TV Rising," *Economist,* Apr. 17, 1993, p. 67). Despite some state concerns regarding the destabilizing potential of unrestricted Western programming (Wong 1993, p. A-17), it seems probable that the regulatory climate for Western-style television advertising in China will remain hospitable.

With specific reference to Asia, Simon Frith observes that

> the technology of advertising tends to be transferred from the West as a complete entity. The implicit theory, practice, values, and attitudes of Western advertising are bundled for export. Thus, the corporate culture within which many Asian advertising messages are developed is inevitably a reproduction of Madison Avenue culture. (quoted in Menon 1993, p. 30)

Since its official reintroduction in 1979, the advertising industry in China has experienced phenomenal levels of growth. Multinational advertisers doubled their ad spending in China from 1992 to 1993, and again by 1994 (Goll 1994, p. B5-A). Total ad spending in China in 1993 increased by 43 percent to $1.9 billion; based on the number of ads appearing, it may already be the second- or third-largest advertising market in the world (Goll 1994, p. B5-A).

Evidence from a variety of sources suggests that consumer advertising in China depends heavily on Western techniques, approaches, and agencies. Chinese ad agencies have learned the importance of psychology from Western practices, and it appears that Chinese ads may well become more subtle, less informational, and more emotion-centered (Stross 1990, pp. 494–5), emulating a process observed earlier in Hong Kong and Taiwan (Tse, Belk, and Zhou 1989). Psychographic and subconscious-oriented advertising will become more prevalent as television replaces billboards as the most popular advertising medium (Bloomberg 1994, sec. 4, p. 4).

Further, the lack of "properly" trained advertising personnel in China ensures a major role for Western agencies in training and educating their Chinese counterparts (Zhou and Belk 1993, pp. 59–60). Among the things Chinese firms have already learned are public relations and apologetic techniques to deflect criticism of advertising, in one case translating and condensing a European ad association pamphlet titled "Ten Questions About Advertising" (Stross 1990, p. 500).

There is reason to believe that advertising in China will continue to grow and continue to adopt the power-knowledge techniques devised by Western agencies. One major force solidly behind the introduction of sophisticated advertising in China is the Chinese government. Several progovernment commentators (summarized in Stross 1990, pp. 489–90) celebrated advertising's ability to "stimulate the consumers' desire to consume" in order to perpetuate expansion of the economy. Indeed, it is clear from a report in the state publication *Beijing Review* that the government, alarmed by commodity stockpiles caused by slackened consumer demand in 1989, increasingly sees advertising as crucial in avoiding such bottlenecks in the future (Yu 1992, p. 11). Truisms such as "pent-up demand" and "natural acquisitiveness," it seems, are no policy substitute in the eyes of Chinese politicians for techniques that manufacture the demand necessary for economic expansion. The government itself is well-positioned both to encourage and benefit from increased advertising in China; the state owns more than 12,000 ad agencies and gains significant foreign exchange from sale of ads on state-run media (Parsons 1993, p. 18). The state Postal Bureau is already a major actor in direct mail advertising, which only began in 1992; by the end of that year, commercial mail accounted for 17 percent of Beijing's total mail (Parsons 1993, p. 19). Finally, through a variety of state and private agencies (closely tied to the regime), the Chinese government continues to import Western advertising expertise and technology (Jianguo 1990, p. 43; Ming 1991, p. 43).

In summary, then, it seems clear that Chinese citizens will continue "learning to want things," with the government, Western firms, and their Chinese junior partners only too happy to teach them how and what to desire, in ever-increasing quantities. The complex of research, multimedia appeals, and feedback loops is well underway toward complete installation in the Chinese context.

Although the technical, institutional, and policy infrastructure is not fully in place outside the advanced industrial countries, there are reasons to believe that, once installed, the consumer-constructing apparatuses may well operate there with fewer restrictions than in their countries of origin. Absent entrenched legacies of privacy rights and other civil protections (which may not be adequate to impede operations even in advanced industrial countries), consumption-generating industries may more freely mix commercial and governmental records, including those gathered for sensitive or "confidential" purposes (a concern shared by Gandy 1993, p. 180).

The impact of the exportation of consumer-creating industries, as part of the more general expansion of global culture industries, is likely to be wide-ranging. A few of the more probable effects can be suggested here:

1. Whatever their other shortcomings, those dependency theorists that earlier focused on the development implications of expanding Western-style consumerism pointed to important relationships. Samir Amin, for example, was among many who suggested that transnational firms, with products developed for core-region middle classes, would likely prefer highly inegalitarian income-distribution policies in Third World regions in order to construct a market segment capable of purchasing their products (1977, p. 9).

If anything, development theory and practice are even more thoroughly affected now by the globalization of production and advertising. Certainly the global culture industries recognize the strategic importance of similar market segments in different regions and cultures—the production of motion pictures, for example, increasingly reflects global marketing strategies (spectacular action pictures à la Schwartzenegger and Stallone move better across cultures than do more nuanced—and culturally bound—character dramas; hence more of the former, less of the latter).

Global advertising agencies recognize similar segments (the product, in part, of prior effects of nonadvertising culture industries). As noted in the 1985 annual report of Saatchi & Saatchi:

> [Today's] sophisticated marketers are recognizing that there are probably more social differences between midtown Manhattan and the Bronx, two sections of the same city, than between Manhattan and the 7th arrondissement of Paris. This means that when a manufacturer contemplates expansion of his business, consumer similarities in demography and habits rather than geographic proximity will increasingly affect his decisions . . . All this underlines the economic logic of the global approach. (quoted in Mattelart 1991, pp. 52–3)

It is in the long-term interest of transnational industries to prompt "consumer similarities in demography and habits" wherever possible. Doing so means greater returns to global rather than local capital, increased returns on initial investment (products/appeals created for one market can be employed in many others), and greater familiarity with and demand for their brands. Generating such standardized consumer segments is a difficult matter, however; hence the interim indispensability of local firms as junior partners (or acquisitions). Still, the quest for globally similar markets—found or created—is likely to continue. It has direct implications for matters of trade and investment policy (openness and globalization over protection and local firms), tax policy (low effective rates on preferred market segments), and many other matters.

2. Similarly, the spread of Western-style consumerist values will affect development decisions concerning public versus private consumption. The products of the global culture industries are nearly uniform in presenting private consumption as normative, normal, and privileged over matters of public consumption (private automobiles are sexy, a city bus is not; successful people generate personal wealth or fame, not public sanitation programs). As they stimulate increased popular demands for private consumption over public goods (public health, housing and schools, communal structures), the consumer-generating industries may become indirect factors impacting matters of state priorities, party platforms, and dissident politics. The privileging of private over collective consumption fits well with, and may generate increased popular support for, the neoliberal policies now unpopular in so many places. These neoliberal policies, like global corporations, seek to privilege consumer rights over citizen rights; to the extent that advertising/marketing industries elevate private consumption and materialism, they may have an impact on this ongoing conflict over the bases of social, moral, and political claims.

The elevation of consumption rights over citizenship rights fits with the preferences of many authoritarian capitalist regimes in poor countries. As James Sterngold notes in the *New York Times*:

> As the 1989 Tiananmen Square crackdown demonstrated, China's Communist Party is far more willing to let citizens choose what they will wear than to select who will lead them or the system under which they will live.
>
> In fact, many argue that the opening of the consumer goods market is intended as a way of deferring political reform. By giving consumers a sense that their lives are improving, and giving them a stake in the status quo, they may not be so eager to demand political change. (Sterngold 1992, p. F-1)

The very concept of development—what is its goal?—is affected if significant groups redefine their primary reference groups, aspirations, and notions of what constitutes a good and meaningful life. If the reference groups derive from global consumption norms, and if notions of a good life presuppose acquisitions and possessions (rather than interpersonal relationships, notions of community, or fidelity to religious values, for example), development will become even more identified with the high-consumption, materialist Western norm—to the exclusion of other, perhaps better, possibilities and at the expense of the physical, social, and moral ecology.

3. Further, to the extent that neoliberal development policies presuppose some sort of political exclusion (given the hardship such policies typically impose on large sectors of the population), the new cultural codes of global capitalism offer another, supplemental basis of exclusion. The latter will be based on access to the latest lifestyle trends and consumption packages proffered by the culture industries—those who have that access will be marked as superior to those lacking them.

Also, given the urban biases of most cultural products, the globalization of such products and marketing techniques are likely to intensify the urban biases of development theory and practice (for one controversial view, see Lipton 1976). As the advertising/marketing industries affect human values, priorities, and ambitions, they may well help stimulate greater rural-to-urban movement (internal migration), with the economic and political strains that produces (the reception of Western-style culture products begins as, and sometimes remains, predominantly urban phenomena in many poor countries). As they convey a greater "familiarity" (however superficial) with core country cultures, they may reduce inhibitions related to external migration to those core countries.

Global culture industries, as they migrate across geographic and cultural distances, confront the Church throughout the entire world. Although the cultural environments of Catholic communities in Rio are not identical to those in Raleigh, some of the most important differences are fading. In particular, Catholic communities throughout the world are coming to move, live, and act in cultural ecologies largely framed and situated by transnational culture industries. Whether the transnational, commercial formation of human communities will meet with responses or resistance from transnational Catholicism remains to be seen. A great deal may depend on how Catholic actors understand the nature of faith, its ongoing transmission and adaptation, and the mission of the Church itself—and how these are impacted by the culture industries.

4

Learning the
Language of Faith

There are at least two ways to envision the previous chapters' issues as of concern to the church. One is superficial and the other is not.

The superficial view sees media oligopoly, the commercial colonization of social and private space, the use of psychological/demographic information, primarily as matters of public policy—to be dealt with alongside other public policy concerns of the church. In this view, the church approaches these issues—housing, aid to poor countries, school lunch programs, health care, and the like—as a more or less coherent entity that interacts, bargains, and compromises with other more or less coherent entities (government agencies, interest groups, research institutes).

When it comes to "global culture industries," the churches thus far have responded with reformist measures that do not disrupt the assumptions or operations of social and political engagement. Lobbying, constituent education, amicus briefs in court cases, and similar measures are most typical. Substantively, the issues are seen to involve matters of media content (sex, violence, and prejudicial stereotyping); matters of media access (the "fairness doctrine," public access requirements in cable franchising); and some concerns for a slightly broader media ownership profile (some restrictions on cross-media ownership, preferential frequency allocations to women and minority groups, nonprofit and community organizations).

Although all of these concerns are legitimate and the means chosen to address them are reasonable, they typify the "missing the forest for the trees" pattern all too typical of much American Christian social engagement. The stakes for the Church *as church* are far higher, the long-term implications far more troubling, than one would assume when treating "global culture industries" as yet another issue area to be dealt with via business-as-usual approaches. In Chapter Six I will discuss in more detail what various church groups have said and done thus far with regard to global culture industries.

My own appraisal can be summarized as follows: The cumulative and interactive effects of global culture industries, the postmodern cultural ecology they shape and that shapes them, and the postfordist political economy to which they are integral, threaten the capacity of the church to survive as a movement committed to a distinctive vision and practice rooted in Christ. Especially (but not exclusively) for the Catholic Church, the ability of the church to reproduce itself in the lives, bodies, and hearts of its members is being undermined at the level of fundamental religious formation. Lobbying for restrictions on sex and violence while the inundation of electronic symbols continues at flood levels is the cultural equivalent of rearranging deck chairs on the *Titanic*; this time, however, the *Titanic* carries the collective attempt to live the gospel in the world.

For my argument to appear plausible, I must first enter the endless debate over what "religion" might mean. As I hope to demonstrate, the most helpful notion of what "religion" might mean is also one in which matters of cultural ecology (and hence global culture industries) are of primary importance. In turn, I suggest that one cannot systematically discount the potential negative consequences of global culture industries and cultural ecology for the church without adopting an inferior, ahistorical idea of "religion."

I enclose the word "religion" in quotation marks here because I am still not sure there is such a thing as religion, recognizable as such across time, space, and cultures. I am strongly, if not yet conclusively, persuaded by scholars that religion as a separate, independently organized segment of life is a creation of Western modernity no more than a few centuries old. People in India, in other words, may not have known that what they "practiced" was a "religion" called "Hinduism"—it was just how they lived, at least until British anthropologists informed them that they had a "religion" called Hinduism (see generally Smith 1963; Asad 1993).

At a minimum, it remains true, as William Paden notes, that the term "religion"

> has become completely equivocal—one word, same sound and spelling, with numerous and different meanings, endlessly flexible. That there has been no agreement on definitions should give one pause. That other cultures do not have a term corresponding exactly to the Western generic *religion* should also give pause. (Paden 1992, pp. 5–6)

So many definitions have been tried and found wanting, and so diverse are the phenomena gathered under the rubric, that the term now is "practically a blank check to be filled in by any interpreter" (Paden 1992, p. 5).

Hence, I intend to do something less than argue for a specific definition of "religion" in what follows; I am suggesting more of a metaphor or analogy than a definition. I am saying that what we in the West call religion "is like" something else we think we understand; that is a more modest claim than to stipulate that religion *is* X or Y or Z. And although I am persuaded that the metaphor or analogy I utilize to understand Christianity also bears fruit for studying other major Western religions, and perhaps even Eastern ones such as Buddhism, Taoism, and Hinduism, I stop short of this larger, all-encompassing claim. Postmodern caution deters me from offering a universal, generic analogy for religion, even if I find it more helpful (in comparative work) than the stronger, definitional universals typical of the modernist era.

After elaborating the understanding of religion and religiosity I find most helpful, I will then close the circle on the issues and processes described in Chapters 2 and 3. With a more adequate understanding of religion in play, Chapter 5 will explore the many ways in which global culture industries undermine the capacity for Christian faith and practice (and I promise to conduct this argument without once complaining about too much sex and violence being the main problem).

It is my fate (occasionally frustrating but often edifying) to work near the citadel of phenomenological, comparativist studies of religion (and Christian theology working with similar concepts). The University of Chicago was and is among the premier places from which phenomenological studies of religion have moved throughout the Western academic world in recent decades. The "Chicago School's" epistemological opposites, from whom I have drawn many of my own notions, are lumped together in the "Yale School," in the jargon of the field.

There is a prevailing assumption—sometimes made explicit, other times only implied—that the Chicago School is better suited for the study and elaboration of matters of concern to Catholics than is the Yale School. The former is said to see continuities (between faith and reason, texts and communities, church and world) more in line with Catholic sensibilities, whereas the latter exaggerates the distance between these in typically Reformed fashion. David Tracy, a leading Catholic scholar in the Chicago School, describes the Yale group as the "second coming of Karl

Barth" (Tracy 1994, p. 310); an admirer has recently described Tracy as "the Schliermacher of our time" (Thistlewaite 1996, p. 225), in reference to the great nineteenth-century liberal Protestant translator of Christianity into categories and concepts comprehensible to secular intellectuals.

Obviously, I am not persuaded that Catholic scholars cannot and should not be informed by insights from the Yale School. Other Catholic scholars are beginning to draw from this intellectual tradition as well (Yamane and Polzer 1994; Buckley 1992; DiNoia 1992; also, similar insights are found in Lohfink 1984, although the genealogy is not identical). To the extent, however, that the "theory of religion" represented by the Chicago School fits comfortably with the intellectual mainstream of American Catholicism, it may add support to my contention that the mainstream rests on unsteady intellectual foundations.

One should not make too much of these divisions—scholars all around continue to challenge and learn from one another, and some are attempting to combine insights from both schools (thus far unsuccessfully, in my view, with Brockelman 1992, as an example). As an approach not wedded to the epistemological foundationalism of modernity, however, I find the Yale School more helpful in more ways than the Chicago-based approaches.

Since I am more interested in exploring the positive and negative features of the Yale approach, I will not present a full critique of the Chicago School except for purposes of contrast. My own understanding has been strongly influenced by *The Nature of Doctrine: Religion and Theology in a Postliberal Age,* published in 1984. This groundbreaking book by George Lindbeck, Pitkin Professor at Yale, has had a modest but steadily increasing impact on ways of understanding religiosity in the social sciences, philosophy, theology, and the humanities. According to one of Lindbeck's critics, this book has become a "seminal text" in the United States, a book "simultaneously a theological critique of secularism, a theological response to Wittgenstein, and a radical statement of the distinctiveness of Christian (and indeed religious) faith and morality" (Gill 1995, pp. 2–3).

Lindbeck first identifies two prior theological and epistemological clusters that have been influential in the past and then offers his own as a third choice. The first of these views religion as a set of propositions that make truth claims about objective realities, similar to philosophy or science as these were traditionally conceived (Lindbeck 1984, p. 16). These propositional theories of religion "have long been on the defensive" during the modern era, while the second theoretical option has gained favor. This second view, the dominant modern theory of religion, is what Lindbeck terms the "experiential-expressive" understanding (Lindbeck 1984, p. 19). Here is where the Chicago School and similar approaches would be situated in Lindbeck's typology.

The Chicago School and other experiential-expressive notions of religion all assume the existence of a human universal known as "religion." They "locate ultimately significant contact with whatever is finally important to religion in the prereflective experiential depths of the soul and regard the public and outer features of religion as expressive and evocative objectifications (i.e., nondiscursive symbols) of internal experience" (Lindbeck 1984, p. 21). Such approaches to religion, preferred by Western liberal thinkers since the time of Schliermacher and into the present, argue that this common, precultural realm of religiosity and religious knowledge/experience remains relatively fixed and stable regardless of what specific turns and twists the local manifestations (e.g., Christianity, Buddhism) of religion might take.

Fergus Kerr, commenting on the distinctions between the Chicago and Yale traditions, notes that

> at Chicago they believe that religion is a universal phenomenon whose rituals and symbols manifest the one same experience of the sacred in different but related ways in different cultural traditions, and Christianity is just one more of these manifestations (no doubt the best one). (Kerr 1994, p. 186)

According to Lindbeck, experiential-expressive approaches to religion gained favor initially at the expense of earlier ideas that saw religion as concerned primarily with empirical truth claims about the real world (what he calls "propositional theories"). At least since Kant, such a picture of religion has been under attack in the West. Phenomenological investigations into "the sacred and the profane" (Eliade), the "idea of the holy" (Otto), and religion in "essence and manifestation" (van der Leeuw) avoided the problems attendant to propositional notions of religion and resonated with modern intellectual sensibilities by focusing on religion as an individualistic, interior-based aspect of human existence. It allowed the study of religion to proceed without undue concern for the fate of religious institutions and practices, given the derivative and (at best) secondary status often (but not always) ascribed to these matters.

These sorts of approaches even allowed for a measure of optimism concerning the future of religion during a time in which older patterns of religious behavior were shifting significantly in the West. If religiosity is first and foremost internal and universal, changes in cultural environments can only affect the external practices and manifestations, and not the "essence" of religion. Modernity may profoundly alter the various expressions of religious sensibilities (less church attendance, sacramental involvement, etc.), postmodern cultural ecology may give prior religious ideas a twirl, but there is no reason to believe the underlying sensibilities are at risk or threatened by *any* change in cultural practices or interactions. Religious institutions might die, but long live religion.

In all of this, there is a provocative, and to my knowledge unexplored, commonality joining the Chicago School of religious studies and the "Chicago Boys" school of economics, whose free-market enthusiasms became elite orthodoxy in Chile and other places. Both parts of the Hyde Park campus argue for an underlying commonality of human nature despite the apparent differences among human cultures; people have a sense of "ultimacy," "the sacred," or the "holy" of a prereflective sort, and people everywhere have a natural propensity to "barter, truck, and exchange" as the Smithian maximizers they are. Both schools would find the first three chapters of this book to be irrelevant, at best, to their concerns, if not downright ludicrous. And each school, incidentally, would probably be mortified to think it had anything in common with the other. Taken together, they represent two strands of a common worldview, what one might call Chicago Orthodoxy—a view of human nature and individualism compatible with the economic and cultural rhythms of capitalist modernity.

In opposition to the religious branch of Chicago Orthodoxy, Lindbeck offers his alternative. Building upon the earlier work of Ludwig Wittgenstein, Clifford Geertz, and others, Lindbeck argues that "religion" is best understood as similar to a cultural-linguistic system:

[A] religion can be viewed as a kind of cultural and/or linguistic framework or medium that shapes the entirety of life and thought . . . It is not primarily an array of beliefs about the true and the good (though it may involve these) or a symbolism expressive of basic attitudes, feelings, or sentiments (though these will be generated). Rather, it is similar to an idiom that makes possible the description of realities, the formation of beliefs, and the experiencing of inner attitudes, feelings, and sentiments. Like a culture or language, it is a communal phenomenon that shapes the subjectivities of individuals rather than being primarily a manifestation of those subjectivities. (Lindbeck 1984, p. 33)

This understanding of religiosity sees the process of becoming religious as similar to that of acquiring a culture or learning a language—that is, "interiorizing outlooks that others have created and mastering skills others have honed" (Lindbeck 1984, p. 22). Like a language or culture, religion remains stubbornly particularistic:

> It is just as hard to think of religions as it is to think of cultures or languages as having a single generic or universal essence of which particular religions—or cultures or languages—are varied manifestations or modifications. One can in this outlook no more be religious in general than one can speak language in general. (Lindbeck 1984, p. 23)

Lindbeck argues that a cultural-linguistic theory of religion is superior to propositional and experiential-expressive theories, while also dealing with the phenomena of most interest in these approaches. For example:

> A comprehensive scheme or story used to structure all dimensions of life is not primarily a set of propositions to be believed, but is rather the medium in which one moves, a set of skills that one employs in living one's life. Its vocabulary of symbols and its syntax may be used for many purposes, only one of which is the formulation of statements about reality. Thus, while a religion's truth claims are often of the utmost importance to it (as in the case of Christianity), it is, nevertheless, the conceptual vocabulary and the syntax or inner logic which determines the kind of truth claims the religion can make. The cognitive aspect, while important, is not primary. (Lindbeck 1984, p. 35)

Comparing his view with the dominant theories of religion, Lindbeck notes:

> Instead of deriving external features of a religion from inner experience, it is the inner experiences which are viewed as derivative . . . There are numberless thoughts we cannot think, sentiments we cannot have, and realities we cannot perceive, unless we learn to use the appropriate symbol systems . . . unless we acquire language of some kind, we cannot actualize our specifically human capabilities for thought, action, and feeling. (Lindbeck 1984, p. 34)

A similar sequencing is suggested by Wayne Proudfoot in his *Religious Experience,* a major work on the matter. To him, religious symbols are not simply expressive or descriptive, but in fact are constructive of religious experience. Such symbolism, to him, is "formative and shapes emotions and experiences. It can be highly evocative and prepare the conditions under which a person will attend to a particular moment and identify that moment as an experience of a certain kind" (1985, pp. 39–40). Lindbeck's linguistic approach to religious (and other sorts of) formation is consistent with that of the later Wittgenstein, who once observed:

> I think there is some truth in my idea that I really only think reproductively. I don't believe that I have ever *invented* a line of thinking, I have always taken one over from someone else . . . What I invent are new similes. (Wittgenstein, quoted in Von Wright and Nyman 1980, p. 19)

The approaches of Lindbeck and similar thinkers strive to move beyond the epistemology of modernity (Lindbeck adopts the term "postliberal" to describe his effort). In this, acknowledges one of his critics, Lindbeck's apparatus is neither static nor conservative, confounding conventional left-right distinctions; although his and related efforts on occasion use the intellectual tools of deconstruction, they are not tied to the nihilistic notions of value attendant to some versions of postmodernism (Tilley 1995, pp. 92, 113).

Closely related to, but not identical with, Lindbeck's notion of religion is the renewed interest in narrative and story as of central importance to religious traditions, theology, and other intellectual disciplines. The "return to narrative" is broad in its sweep, influencing both the humanities and social sciences (Maines 1993). It has emerged as a corrective to modernist assumptions of autonomous and self-forming individuals, detached rational-action decisionmaking, and fact-value distinctions.

According to Alasdair MacIntyre,

> it is through hearing stories about wicked stepmothers, lost children, good but misguided kings, wolves that suckle twin boys, youngest sons who receive no birthright but must make their own way in the world, and eldest sons who waste their inheritance on riotous living and go into exile to live with the swine that children learn or mislearn both what a child is and what a parent is, what the cast of characters may be in the drama into which they have been born and what the ways of the world are. Deprive children of stories and you leave them unscripted, anxious stutterers in their actions as in their words. (MacIntyre 1981, pp. 216)

According to one voice in narrative theology:

> Our lives are shaped more by models, metaphors, stories, and myths than by abstract sets of rules and principles. We try to become like certain types of persons whose way of life appeals to us. Our actions tend to be imitative of individuals rather than guided by rules. They are imitative of those individuals whose excellence and attainments please and inspire them; consequently, they participate in the same intentionality and orientations. (Navone 1990, p. 50)

In religious traditions, only certain stories are considered normative and crucial for the faith—Christianity has not relied on stories of the Buddha, nor did the Lakota initially need stories of Jacob and Esau. As John Navone notes:

> The life story of Jesus Christ and his Church is paradigmatic for the Christian lived-understanding of our own God-self-neighbor relationship. Theology is a systematic articulation of this story, of the Christian myth: the truth by which a Christian believes that he must live, the story that is normative for judging the true meaning and value of every human life story. Christian faith is the acceptance of the summons to live by the truth of Jesus Christ's life story as the way to becoming our true selves. (Navone 1990, p. xv).

It is no coincidence that discipleship models of Christian life often go hand in hand with theological epistemologies that stress the centrality of narrative—the works of James William McClendon, Ched Myers, and Stanley Hauerwas are only a few examples of this convergence. Navone expresses this point of view (although I do not find it at all as widely shared as he suggests):

> The Christian community generally agrees that the influence of Jesus on life and action is what counts. Christianity is constituted by the personal continuity of Jesus' action, by the sharing of his interiority, his intention with others . . . An authentic Christian is a person who shares and continues in his own life the intention and activity of Christ . . . Hence, to discover whether individuals or institutions are Christian we must know whether they share the historic continuity of purpose and intention uniquely expressed in the life of Jesus and first defined by him in his teaching. (Navone 1990, p. 92)

Attention to the tradition's central stories not only orients its members' individual and collective lives, it also provides a basis for ongoing self-assessment and critique, "a means of asking the hard questions about the community's own faithfulness" (Hauerwas, Murphy, and Nation 1994, p. 23).

A critical area that Lindbeck and the narrativists draw attention to is the central importance of emotions, affectivity, and dispositions in the structuring of religiosity and faith. Martha Nussbaum is among many who argue that emotions are themselves narratively constructed; they are not feelings that well up in a "natural" and untutored way. Rather, people "learn how to feel in and through the narratives of particular societies" (Nussbaum 1989, pp. 217).

Such a view is echoed by Richard B. Steele:

> It is not simply the case that Scripture simply *stipulates* what emotions ought to characterize Christian faith. It also *displays* them in its "giants and heroes" and *elicits* them from its faithful readers. And precisely here we may observe the shrewd psychological insights of the biblical authors. They apparently understood that one cannot simply tell people to *feel* thus and so, as one can sometimes tell people to *do* this or that. If one wants them to cultivate a particular emotion, one must shape the judgments which are entailed in that emotion, and more importantly, one must excite their *interest* in the object of that emotion. (Steele 1994, p. 174)

Attending to the role of emotion and affectivity is a strength of Lindbeck's concept of religiosity. Those approaches he characterizes as expressive-experiential have been criticized, especially by feminist scholars (e.g., Parsons 1995), for neglecting the importance of emotions, in favor of an autonomous, disconnected "rational" self that operates via rule-based ethics. Joseph DiNoia suggests that modernist approaches like these "fail to account for this inextricable connection between the particular aims of life commended by religious communities and the specific sets of dispositions they foster to promote the attainment and enjoyment of those aims" (1990, p. 257).

Narrative, a cultural-linguistic sense of religion, and the rejection of foundationalist accounts of secular and religious knowledge—such are the bases, broadly considered, of the Yale School as I see it. Such a summary statement risks conveying a sense of unanimity, of smooth conceptual integration, whereas in fact scholars working in these areas struggle together to discern linkages, implications, and gaps. Within this broad gathering of voices, some cautions and reservations can be heard. Hauerwas suggests that Lindbeck's schema focus on only a handful of theories of religion and doctrine, although more may exist (Hauerwas and Jones 1989, p. 7); he also suggests that some advocates of narrative methodologies are guilty of seeing them as panaceas, *the* solution to intellectual problems confronting the church and the post-Enlightenment world (Hauerwas and Jones 1989, p. 1–4).

Less sympathetic critics are easily found, challenging cultural-linguistic understandings of Christianity and the importance of primary narratives therein. Their concerns are various. While not exhaustive, the following is a representative sampling of major criticisms.

Terence Tilly faults Lindbeck and the narrative theologians for under-estimating the constancy of intra-Christian pluralism and for providing inadequate ways to privilege one Christian narrative over others. He also finds Lindbeck's call for Christians to live more "intratextually," more with dispositions, priorities, and images drawn from the biblical world, to be naive; people cannot live only within the constructed world of Scripture, but in fact are formed by many interpenetrating worlds. Finally, he finds Lindbeck weak on matters of institutions and community, a surprise given the irreducibly social nature of Lindbeck's argument (1995, pp. 101, 104–5, 109, 111).

Robin Gill finds Lindbeck's cultural-linguistic approach applicable, if at all, only to text-based religions; it doesn't work well for understanding orally or aesthetically based religious traditions nor for those Christian eras in which illiteracy was the norm. He also suggests that these approaches unnecessarily exaggerate the differences between church and world and embody a temptation toward coercion to eliminate the plurality of stories typical of all religious traditions.

David Tracy agrees with narrativists like Hans Frei that "God's identity is Christianly established in and through the passion narrative's rendering of the identity of and presence of Jesus as the Christ." He says that Frei and others are less persuasive in arguing that Luke's sort of realistic, history-like narrative is sufficient for the Christian naming of God. The Gospels of Mark, Matthew, and John do not work nearly as well for such purposes, Tracy argues, whereas John and the Pauline corpus are more appropriate for the analogical or dialectical naming of God (1994, pp. 310–2).

Glen Stassen finds the narrative school deficient in dealing with matters of justice; this is a blind spot Stassen would remedy with recourse to the work of Michael Walzer (1994, pp. 204, 208–12).

Finally, Janet Soskice gives voice to the concern that Lindbeck and the narrativists may represent a threat to the newly emergent theologies of women, the poor, minorities, and marginal groups. Who will tell the stories? who builds communities? are the communities voluntary or not? how are dissenters handled?—these are just some of the hard questions that emerge, even if one assumes that Lindbeck is basically correct (an assumption Soskice does not offer). She notes that feminists are both attracted and repelled by the emphases on narrative, community, and the postmodern (1995, pp. 16–7).

It is not my place to defend Lindbeck and the narrativists from their critics—they have done so frequently and, in my view, in a generally (but not completely) satisfactory manner (for an overview of the debates, see Lints 1993, and Stell 1993). What I observe about the many criticisms outlined above is that none of them—except Gill's charge of text-only relevance—challenges the fundamental epistemology of cultural-linguistic understandings. Few seem prepared to argue for notions of religiosity as presocial, prelinguistic, or individualistic in nature. And few seem to dispute the contention that human dispositions, values, and conceptual grammars are the product of interactions in which cultural institutions, socialization, and the like play major roles. The criticisms here are more concerned with how real-life religious groups manage, reformulate, fight about, and advocate within and between narrative postures. These are important questions, but they are not intractable *ab initio*; neither do they undermine the cogency of cultural-linguistic approaches to faith. They mostly point to the enduring presence of conflict and power in all human collective enterprises—religious communities being no exception.

Among the specific criticisms listed above, several are weak and easily addressed. Contrary to Tilley's assumption, Lindbeck never assumes that believers can live only in a world constructed by the Bible; indeed, a major concern in *The Nature of Doctrine* is the extent to which other cultural-linguistic "worlds" (the market, technical rationality, individualism) have undercut processes of *any* gospel-based individual and group formation. Stassen's claim that narrative theology neglects social justice concerns seems to be a product of incomplete reading; theologians such as Brueggemann and Myers, who explicate the narratives of the Hebrew Scriptures and New Testament, put the texts' distinctive ideas of social justice at the *center* of their work—Walzer's contribution seems tame by comparison. Gill's objection that Lindbeck exaggerates the differences between Christianity and the world says more about Gill's more accommodationist ecclesiology than about any basic deficiencies in Lindbeck's work. And there is no automatic or inevitable path that leads from a regard for narrative and cultural-linguistic theories of religion to coercive responses to plurality or dissent—such an argument is infused by faulty logic and buttressed by past failures of the church to deal with internal differences in a Christian manner.

The weakest criticism, ironically, is the one focusing most fundamentally on the cultural-linguistic approach. Gill claims that Lindbeck's cultural-linguistic framework involves attention only to literary, written texts and their role in religiosity. "There have after all been forms of Christian community, especially before the ages of the printed word, which have known very little about the Bible. Presumably on Lindbeck's theory they must almost be disallowed as being 'Christian.'" Against canonical scripture, Gill offers worship as "the most distinctive feature of Christianity," "a feature that characterizes all churches in all ages." It may even be the case, says Gill, that "it is worship which gives substance to religious language and which is a key feature in doctrinal formulation" (1995, pp. 8–9).

Gill's objections are easily met. First, Lindbeck's explication of cultural-linguistic processes do *not* limit him only to the written word as being significant for religious communities—he specifically notes the importance of aesthetic and nondiscursive symbols as significant components of "language." The aesthetic, nondiscursive aspects of religion (e.g., poetry, music, art, ritual) are not externals or peripherals to Lindbeck. "Rather, it is through these that the basic patterns of religion are interiorized, exhibited, and transmitted" (1984, pp. 35–6).

With art, architecture, and performative expression part of the linguistic universe (a point explored with particular effectiveness by Goethals 1990), Gill's opposition of "scripture" to "worship" appears false. For what, after all, does most Christian worship express if not the stories, characters, and images derived or developed from those of Jesus and the Bible? Although Lindbeck does concentrate on the canonical scriptures, his cultural-linguistic frame can in no way be construed as a writing-only theory. This is a puzzling argument, given the ease of its refutation.

Several other concerns I find to be more legitimate and deserving extended attention, even though they do not strike at the epistemological foundations of the approach. These concern matters of internal pluralism, the pluralism presented in scripture and tradition, questions of religious authority and freedom, and the capacity for once-silenced groups to tell the Christian stories in their own fashion. These questions rest at the heart of debates within Catholicism and the Christian world on matters involving the Petrine office and magisterium, unity and diversity of theological expression, and the globalization of the faith. I share the desire for inclusiveness, a diversity of voices telling the Christian story; however, I do not agree with critics who suggest that greater attention to the narrative quality of faith requires papal authoritarianism, inquisitorial discipline, or similar straitjackets. Cultural-linguistic and narrative approaches say that the range of "Christian" stories is not infinite; it does not follow that there is only one version that can or should be told, heard, and lived. It *does* follow that many of the debates in question presuppose some common grammar of faith for the necessary debates to be intelligible or minimally productive. The outcomes of the debate are not rigged in advance if one takes Lindbeck's approach seriously; it does help participants focus on primary differences, as well as primary agreements, within the same religious worlds.

Considerable benefit continues to accrue from Christian feminist and liberationist biblical scholarship and theology as they continue to discover, excavate, reconstruct, and articulate stories of faith neglected or suppressed in favor of others. I see no conflict between my work and scholars in these fields—indeed, I see them as mutually supportive in reclaiming versions of the gospel more radical in their implications. The centrality of the Jesus narratives in the work of liberation theologians like Jon Sobrino and Leonardo Boff is one example of this (e.g., Boff 1978; Sobrino 1978, 1987).

For the Christian faith to exist at all, it must be transmitted, passed on, received, and lived. These are intrinsically social and cultural processes, dependent upon skills and structures akin to those of language. If these are impeded, obscured, overwhelmed, or undermined, Christian faith—of any kind—grinds to a halt.

5

How Global Culture Industries
Undermine Christianity

Having been accustomed to the easy-fitting notion of Church that is contemporary Catholicism in advanced industrial countries, it is sometimes hard to understand that people used to be turned away from Church membership. In earlier times, those whose motives were suspect, who seemed not to grasp the radical transformations of life and attitude required by the Christian life, who were not sufficiently grounded in Scripture and the life of the church, were told, "Not yet. You need more preparation."

Such was the experience of the early church, in which would-be members underwent a lengthy formation period (usually lasting three years or more). During this time, they would learn of the Christian life by imitating a teacher; their participation in the Church was only partial, with greater inclusion following evidence of progress made in reshaping one's self in the ways of Christ. These learners, called catechumens, were excused from the worship service before the Eucharist began—the most precious of Christian devotional practices was reserved for the baptized, those whose lives had already been given over to Christ and the Kingdom. Making a Christian was seen as a process requiring much time, a gradual exposure to those practices and doctrines central to the Christian movement, and the systematic weaning from non-Christian values, practices, and priorities. Each catechumen, in other words, was "converted" into a Christian, a disciple of the Way.

In many ways, processes of Christian lay formation were best exemplified during this period of late antiquity. Subsequent changes and compromises—the accommodation with the Roman Empire, the abandonment of the catechumenate and moves toward easy admission policies, and the rise of clericalism—diluted the processes by which would-be Christians were converted in their affections, actions, and commitments. If we wish to understand how Christians were made in a time when doing so was a high priority (and not merely for those within religious orders or the clerical caste), we today can learn from the practices of the early church. The point is not to ape our predecessors, but rather to see what might be necessary for the gospel—then as now, a radical call to conversion—to pass from believers to would-be believers, transforming human hearts and lives toward alignment with the priorities and commitments of Jesus. Our current context—a cultural ecology producing and produced by capitalist globalization—is such that we have more to learn from eras in which Christian formation was a central priority for the church than when it was something de-emphasized, left primarily to underprepared families, or entrusted to nonecclesial institutions and processes.

As noted by Navone, the four Gospels were used by the early church as manuals of instruction for the formation of members both before and after baptism. Mark's gospel was usually the first an initiate encountered, the "gospel of the catechumen"; it was used to lead people with inchoate religious stirrings toward Christian ones. In particular, it was used to challenge and replace the seeker's notions of God with those relevant to knowing God's grace through Jesus and discipleship.

> In this first phase, Catechumens must abandon the popularly accepted stereotypes of divine power and human success, the image of a god made to the measure of their self-interest and suited to their personal ease or comfort. Catechumens cannot have a risen Lord without a suffering Messiah; they cannot have a lived experience of God's love for us in Jesus Christ without walking his road of suffering self-transcendence. (Navone 1990, p. 14)

The Gospel of Matthew, called "the gospel of the catechist," was used to help the newly baptized mature in the practice of his or her faith. The community typically used five standards in assessing the newly baptized's "degree of participation" to date in the discipleship community of the Church (Navone 1990, p. 14):

- to have brought forth fruits of the Kingdom (21:43);
- to have done the will of God (5:16, 7:21);
- attaining the higher righteousness (5:20);
- shaping one's life in order to enter the Kingdom (7:13); and
- good works to glorify God (5:16).

Luke-Acts was a two-volume manual for the third phase of Christian maturation for Christians who, "already adhering to Jesus Christ and his community, are seeking to grasp their meaning for the world." This phase also involved learning to explain and defend the faith in a world of Greek, Roman, and Jewish suspicion and persecution; at this stage, members learned that "to explain oneself to others, one must first be able to understand oneself: one must be able to tell one's own story" (Navone 1990, pp. 15–6).

Finally, the abstract, highly theological Gospel of John represented the challenge and nurture of the community's elders and wise ones. In this context, John's gospel "represents the culmination of the foundational experience of God's love in Jesus Christ and his community, of an all-embracing, universal love to be preached to all nations."

> It represents the simplicity of vision of one who has mastered the complexity of the three Synoptic manuals and their corresponding horizons . . . John synthesizes the entire Christian experience in terms of the gift of God's love in Jesus Christ and his Spirit. The Church's confession of faith, Eucharist, fellowship, gospels, prayers, precepts, proclamation, rites, service, and witness are called into existence and sustained by the gift of this love that alone constitutes their true meaning and value . . . John, the manual of Christian wisdom, promotes an integrated vision of the entire Christian experience in both its internal (Church) and external (world) relationships. (Navone 1990, p. 16)

Whatever variations local churches practiced in the pre-Constantinian era, the formation of church members was generally a matter of great seriousness. It seemed to require:

- a substantial investment of time on the part of the initiate and the community;
- a process of *sequential learning*, with knowledge building upon knowledge and practice upon practice. People gradually developed the religious competencies and appetites necessary to appreciate and benefit from later practices and lessons. There remained reserved knowledge and practice, things for which the initiated had to demonstrate themselves adequately prepared and formed;
- an apprenticeship with a church member, with the latter acting as an exemplar or role model for the neophyte. Processes of mimetic, or imitative learning, seemed of central importance;

- materials of instruction, most of which (as suggested by Navone and others) were steeped in narratives of Jesus, stories of Israel and the church, and parables of the Kingdom;
- formal examination of candidates, with rejection a live possibility;
- obligations on the receiving community to live up to the standards expected of the catechumen and to walk with the newly baptized along the path of discipleship;
- a developed capacity for an interior spiritual life—in other words, the ability to pray as a Christian.

With such a process of formation as that of the early church, one could learn the faith (or a foreign language, to use Lindbeck's metaphor) and come to inhabit its world. With such a formation process, I suspect, one could learn just about anything. But in our day, amidst the ceaseless flow of television, ubiquitous advertising and marketing messages, and interwoven data networks, processes of making Christians in a serious way are severely compromised.

In Chapter Three, I discussed some aspects of "postmodern" culture associated with postfordist capitalism, initially with reference to advertising/marketing as a major sector in the global culture oligopoly. I want to enhance and expand that picture here by drawing attention to how contemporary cultural ecology renders serious Christian formation ever more difficult. To do so requires special attention to the most important sector of global culture industries in the West, namely television.

Living in Television's World

In my view, the most pernicious aspect of television in advanced industrial societies is that it seems so normal. It doesn't seem odd, alien, or strange—indeed, it's part of the living room, a reliable and unexceptional part of daily life. In less than fifty years, television seems indispensable to life in postmodern America (certainly more important than indoor plumbing or flush toilets, judging by the numbers). We are perfectly at home with a social phenomenon that, were we to describe it to someone with no knowledge of it, would either sound strange in itself or would make the people cohabiting with television sound strange.

Under the banner of cultural studies and the self-promotion of the culture industries, television-bashing has acquired a bad name in recent years. While I do not claim that television is all-powerful, I do want to rehabilitate the honorable practice of television-bashing. More specifically, I want to acknowledge, and encourage others to contemplate, the huge transformative impact that television has had on everyday life and most people in advanced industrial countries. Doing so becomes increasingly more difficult with each passing day. As noted by Alan Olson,

> the psychological disjunction between the world *before* and the world *after* television is so vast that critical issues regarding the nature and meaning of the medium are difficult to identify, much less address and resolve. Indeed, we are rapidly approaching a time in which there will be no living memory of a world before this medium; hence, we are not able to see the forest for the trees with respect to the task of criticism. (Olson 1991, p. 1)

What, after all, is television? Stripped down, it might be described as

- a highly centralized, overwhelmingly one-way transmission vector that reaches into the private living space of nearly every man, woman, and child in the United States, Japan, and Western Europe;
- the central social institution in those regions for disseminating and validating common stories, symbols, sounds, pictures, information, "news," values, frames of reality, and social archetypes;
- a major advertising/marketing instrument through which the attention of audiences of different demographic types are assembled (via program offerings and variations), processed into modes of consciousness receptive to commercial messages (via the tone, pacing, and sequencing of those program offerings), and sold to corporations (who pay different rates for access to different sorts of audiences).

With regard to the matters at hand, one of the strangest things is how little thought has been given to television's effects upon religious communities. Although a few scholars have ventured into the topic, it remains largely unexplored territory (Arthur 1995). Persons looking for conventional behavioral or social scientific "evidence" on the question are likely to be disappointed. The absence of literature emerges, I suspect, from two powerful yet divergent assumptions extant in the academic world: one assumes the declining significance or importance of religion (the secularization theorists, past and present variants); the other assumes the general constancy of religion in human communities (the Chicago School being one variant of this). Scholars impressed by the first assumption would see media effects as but a subset of larger secular trends ("modernization"), whereas those working with the second would not expect cultural ecology to change anything but the surface particulars of religious experience.

To argue as I do, that global culture industries influence significantly the maintenance and reproduction of the Christian community, is necessarily an argument built at least in part on speculative materials. If Christianity as a lived and incarnate movement transmits its heritage in the ways I think it does and if major culture industries work as I suggest they do in this chapter and earlier ones, then it does not seem unreasonable to suggest conflicts in their fundamental cognitive, communal, and psychosocial processes. In this conflict, I argue that thus far the powers of religious formation have been overmatched by the formative capacities of television and other culture industries.

Although other analysts have sought to argue that religious formation remains healthy and well, much of that literature sees conventional behavioral or ideological evidence (church attendance, reported belief in God, etc.) as proof of the enduring effectiveness of religious socialization (e.g., Greeley 1993). At the other end, media apologists and some scholars in the cultural studies movement have gone to great lengths to deny that culture industries (television, advertising) have *any* "power" or socially significant effects. The transparency of this second literature is most in evidence when it resorts to debunking the straw-man "hypodermic" model of media effects (discussed with reference to advertising in Chapter Three; see Schudson 1984 as an example of "disproving" media power with such tactics). The debate will doubtless continue, and corporate media representatives will continue their Janus-faced discourse: for example, denying any significant effects of television when testifying before Senate panels investigating sex and violence on the screen, only to argue for the effectiveness of TV when pitching ad time to corporations. Although I object to the worldview and priorities of corporate executives as a group, I do not think they are fools; I do not think they have been duped into spending $150 billion a year in U.S. advertising that has no effect in the face of "consumer sovereignty," "active audiences," or any other self-congratulatory label of the day.

I am aware of the impossibility of offering conclusive "proof" or "evidence" regarding the effects of television on Christian formation. The problems here are both theological and epistemological. If one's expectations of what Christianity should be are appropriately modest, one sees nothing drastically wrong with the religious status quo and therefore no troubling effects on formation from culture industries. On the other hand, if you deny that global culture industries have effects or processes similar to those I describe, then you won't be persuaded that the culture industries are part of the problem facing the church. Persons in either of these camps will insist on "evidentiary" standards that cannot be attained in this or any other analysis of this sort (on the more fundamental epistemological questions, see Kuhn 1970; Bernstein 1971; Simon 1982). Nevertheless, I offer the following assessment in hopes of providing a useful interpretation of how global culture industries interact with processes of religious formation.

Restricting myself primarily to television, I discuss several aspects of its operation in advanced industrial countries that are inimical to the formation of Christian convictions, affections, and practices. I need only outline a few of them to suggest how television and other culture industries subvert the processes of acquiring Christian "language" and habits.

The Attractiveness of Television

The products of global culture industries are attractive, none more so than television. It is a cliché that television no longer *conveys* culture but has supplanted it; like most clichés, this one is grounded in experience.

Many of the numbers are familiar in broad outline, but they should remain astounding in spite of that. People in North America, Western Europe, and Japan spend between 20 and 33 percent of their waking lives watching television, more than any single waking-hours activity except working for money (unless considering the unemployed or underemployed, most of whom spend more time watching television than working) (Murray-Brown 1991, p. 19). Young people watch between 20 and 25 hours of television per week, in addition to 20 hours per week of radio listening; adults seem to average slightly higher radio involvement and slightly lower television viewing, but the differences are modest (21 hours per week of television watching, for instance; see Ekstrom 1992, p. 135).

Intense involvement with television and other electronic entertainment media seems to be established early in childhood in advanced industrial countries. Children ages 2 to 5 watch TV 4 hours per day on average, those 6 to 11 watch 3½ hours per day (Jacobson and Mazur 1995, p. 22). One-third of kids under 17 watch 5 hours or more of TV daily, and the average child will have logged between 19,000 and 24,000 hours of television time before his or her 19th birthday. That compares to approximately 12,000 hours of schooling if he or she does not drop out before completing high school (systems such as the Chicago Public Schools have dropout rates approaching 50 percent) (Ekstrom 1992, p. 135). Today's teenagers, assuming a 75-year life span, may spend nearly 13 years of their lives watching television—3 years of which will have been commercials. Children see 2 to 3 hours of television ads per week, or about 40,000 TV commercials a year (Jacobson and Mazur 1995, p. 41). Even if viewers are not always "attentive" to television at all times, their involvement with it remains immense.

So attractive is television viewing in advanced industrial countries that *not* watching large amounts of television is the exception. As one scholar observes:

> I have had students who describe people who don't own a television set as deviants, fit for the madhouse; and of course it is true that if you don't view on a regular basis, you are a cultural oddity, not properly in tune with the times. You are deprived, or backward, in a new kind of way, as were illiterates in print culture. (Murray-Brown 1991, p. 20)

The future may bring an intensification of these trends. Amidst the hype of the "information superhighway" Tom Frank notes that the most likely effect of interactive media (including television) will be to increase people's temporal and emotional investment in commercial media (1995, p. 7).

It seems that people love television or at least have strong investments of time with it (verging on addictive behaviors for a substantial portion of the population). Why do people in advanced industrial countries watch so much television?

Many accounts of the rising popularity of television viewing focus on macrosociological factors—increased social mobility, the instability of local communities and neighborhoods, the erosion of familial ties, fear of crime, and the low monetary costs of television viewing relative to other pursuits. Although these sorts of factors are relevant in varying degrees, too often the reciprocal effects of television viewing on these phenomena have not been explored adequately—that is, whether rising levels of television consumption affect factors like the aforementioned (an exception, in part, is the "cultivation effect" theory and Cultural Indicators project developed by George Gerbner, Michael Morgan, Nancy Signorelli, and others). Only in recent years have sociological factors been supplemented by sustained attention to television as a phenomenon with significant emotional, cognitive, physiological, and psychological implications. These latter concerns, I will argue, are crucial in assessing the prospects for Christian formation in television-drenched cultures.

For all the discussion about television content, it begins first of all as combinations of light and sound. Particularly in its visuality, television seems ideally suited to invite and hold human attention. Some scholars argue that attentiveness to visuality is innate in the human brain, related to the exigencies of hunting, self-protection, and other tasks requiring the ability to recognize minute changes in visual field. As Renée Hobbs, the director of Harvard's media studies center concludes, the impact of television on attention

> bears a close relationship to what we know about the human perceptual system. Our eyes are designed to actively monitor change. It is built-in, hard-wired, as it were, into the perceptual system. Younger children don't have very much control over using the perceptual system, and so they are compelled to watch the intense movement on the screen. Although over time we gain control, even adults find this array of excitement and visual changes on the TV screen compelling . . . Sometimes, no matter how interesting the conversation might happen to be, no matter how much you wanted to participate in the conversation, you found your eyes being drawn inexplicably to the screen. It is an attentional behavior that even adults find difficult to control. (Hobbs 1991, pp. 36–7)

Enhancing television's innate attractiveness to the human perceptual complex are editing conventions (close-ups, zooms, long shots, panning shots) that "may themselves be perceptual analogues of mental processes, which may explain why it is so easy to watch television" (Hobbs 1991, p. 34).

The editing conventions of television are intended to avoid "visual boredom," produced by a lack of exciting images or sounds. It is the need for "good television" that avoids boredom that typifies television as developed under commercial auspices in the United States (and which has come to displace competing television norms all over the world); and it is the commercial demand to keep audiences for as long as possible that explains television's focus on emotion—fear, excitement, passion, surprise, lust. Jeremy Murray-Brown argues that the central form of television is drama and that drama inherently focuses (and acts upon) human emotion:

In itself a television image [that never changes] is dull. It is so lacking in arousal that we need exaggerated sound and devices like the [editing] cut to maintain interest . . .

   Given the choice between two visual images, we will always take the stronger, the more dramatic one. What is transmitted through this form, therefore, is predominantly emotional information. Eliminate these dramatic devices and you have no program. In fact, you don't have what we mean by "television." Nothing is more boring than a camera that never changes its angle or shot, nothing less likely to attract an audience, and so less capable of sending messages. (Murray-Brown 1991, pp. 23, 25)

The strong affinities between the formal structures of television and human perceptual processes help account for the ease of television watching. It also seems to be the case that, owing to the same sorts of factors that make viewing seem "natural," human perceptual processes and dispositions are themselves changed by television conventions.

On the first point, research on a community's first exposure to television (a dying field if there ever was one) provides some provocative insights. Reflecting on her experiences with a Kenyan people with no prior exposure to television, Hobbs found that

with no experience with the medium, these villagers were perfectly adept at decoding this media specific symbol system, namely, point-of-view narration. Based on our research, we believe that some editing conventions are perceptual isomorphs of experience; you don't need experience with the medium to decode them. This explains why television is so easy to watch, why it takes so little effort for us to decode, why it takes no mental effort to watch television. From this it follows that the representational codes of film and television can also help to develop or degenerate the cognitive skills of attention, comprehension, interpretation, and prediction. (Hobbs 1991, pp. 34–5)

Comparable insights emerge from the important study of television by Joshua Meyrowitz:

In contrast to reading and writing, television watching involves an access code that is barely a code at all. Television by no means presents "reality," but television looks and sounds much more like reality than sentences and paragraphs do. Even two-year-old children find television accessible, and this explains why television is so readily used as a "baby sitter." Children aged two to five watch over twenty-five hours of television per week. These active television watchers are of an age when the letters of the alphabet are little more than odd shapes and lines—except, perhaps those dynamic letters that are pictured on "Sesame Street"....

In general, there is no set sequence in which television programs must be watched. A person does not necessarily have to watch "simple programs" before watching "complex programs" . . . There are no specific "prerequisites" for watching a television program, as there are prerequisites for reading *Ulysses*. While the complexity of the *content* of television may vary, the ways in which the content is *encoded* in different television programs is relatively constant: pictures and sound. The often-used phrase "visual literacy," therefore, is a misnomer. Understanding visual images has nothing to do with literacy. (Meyrowitz 1985, pp. 76–7)

Other analysts, including Postman (1985), make similar points.

Regarding the second point, the fragmentation of images, messages, and sounds that emerges from television's structured reach for emotional impact seems to change how television viewers perceive nontelevision phenomena:

Because we are used to receiving fragmented information and information in discontinuous form, we come to prefer that form; and information, such as a formal lecture, that requires sustained attention over a long period of time becomes more difficult because it is not habitually required in our culture. Consequently, it takes a great deal more effort and discipline to make the attitudinal adjustment to a formal lecture of 60 minutes or more, for it is an adjustment that runs against the grain of discontinuity. (Hobbs 1991, pp. 37–8)

The disjointed, fragmented nature of televisual processes leaves large gaps of meaning that must be filled by audiences in the act of viewing. Over time, according to Robert Scholes (1991, pp. 83–6), people find such assemblages to be pleasurable—an acquired pleasure, no doubt, but one for which we seem willing to sacrifice huge chunks of our life's attention and time. And with so much time spent watching television, and with the cognitive-perceptual habits of most people shaped in accordance with that medium, other forms of social communication have been forced to change to accommodate these new habits of reception—a process recognized by Postman a decade ago. Viewers (in other words, virtually all of us) have taken to television so thoroughly that,

> in other words, television format has determined public expectations regarding all formats, at least for the mass public, which itself influences the elite public more than we would like to admit. Television formats not only influence television but all other aspects of culture. It is precisely in this sense that formats and editing conventions have their greatest power. (Hobbs 1991, p. 43)

A culture in which television is dominant and preferred is one immersed in video experience, which "avoids the dull end of the interest spectrum characteristic of lived experience by employing formal features—compression, ellipsis, inserts, montage—which function to sustain viewers' interests . . . They alter the pace of lived experience, while preserving the sense of both lived experience's continuity and video experience's depictive character" (Hobbs, 1991, p. 57).

Overall, then, it seems possible to explain the attractiveness and addictiveness of television viewing with relatively little emphasis on the specifics of television programming. As Murray-Brown concludes, "the affective quality of television lies in its technology. Its forms are educating as much as its content. It is the act of viewing that attracts viewers rather than specific programs" (1991, p. 22). It remains true that in the United States, for example, most people watch television by the clock instead of by the program, and most are surprisingly undemanding with regard to what they will watch (Meyrowitz 1985, p. 84). Hence, while the specifics of television programming are important, they seem to be of a secondary nature; religious programming or pornography, educational children's television or slasher films—beneath the topical differences are important commonalities of pace, audio-visual excitement, editing conventions, and other means of audience enticement.

Into the Flood

Television has demonstrated its capacity, like other popular culture industries, to attract and hold human attention. What began as a trickle of television two generations ago (other media have their own genealogy) has now reached flood stage—inundating viewers and nonviewers alike, 24 hours a day every day, in all spaces and places of our lives. Led by television, the images, sounds, enticements, and reminders of commercial culture surround us and our families without respite, sanctuary, or refuge.

Due to the increased importance of culture industries in late capitalism (as discussed in Chapters Two and Three), we can expect the flood of mediated images, sales pitches, and entertainments to continue unabated. Television, for example, has proven itself to be such an effective marketing tool that governments worldwide have been pressed to deregulate (making available more frequencies, eliminating many content requirements) and privatize (more commercial channels, more narrowcasting formats, more commercially driven content and ads). With dozens of channels (perhaps to reach the hundreds, if enthusiasts are to be listened to) operating nonstop day and night, the medium needs raw cultural material like a vampire needs fresh blood. New stories, novel images, unexpected recombinations of the familiar, outrageous juxtapositions, assaults on conventional norms, seductive appeals, and audience flattery—such is the problematic of television in postmodern capitalism, where the proliferation of stations and lengthening of the broadcast day bring the questions: How to break through the clutter? How to draw in audiences who have seen nearly everything, bought nearly everything, been disappointed by nearly everything?

One can see in television a trait shared by most for-profit culture industries. It is omnivorous. Industry representatives and "creatives" prowl the world for programming ideas, exotica, spectacles, sounds, dramas, pathos—anything to *entice viewers* and *fill airtime*. Because television audiences in advanced capitalist countries have experiential bases limited increasingly to and by what they see on television, novelty and the exotic must often be joined with the familiar, the warmly remembered, the unthreatening. Programming must be different enough to draw a crowd but not so different as to frighten viewers or remind them of their own ignorance or limited horizons. Even old television programming can serve as a secure anchor through which to attract current audiences—endless reruns, updates, and revivals of old sitcoms being the most apparent examples of this rather sad practice.

It is the need to fill the airtime and draw the viewers with the unexpected that accounts for television's blender-like effects of past and existing cultures—aspects from living or once-living cultures are appropriated (music, dance, dress, language, story), recombined and reshuffled with wildly dissimilar or contradictory cultural artifacts, and used to draw people to a sales pitch (or are themselves sales pitches). This is one way to generate what the theorists call decontextualization and fragmentation, among the defining elements of postmodern cultural ecology. Decontextualization means spectacles (war, famine, urban violence) without history or memory; fragmentation means disconnected images, sounds, and representations following one another, or occurring simultaneously, with no evident coherence of purpose, meaning, or interrelation (save for enticing and intriguing viewers).

Like nature's deluges, the culture industry flood respects no limits of space or separation unless forced to yield. Television is the cornerstone of the spatial expansion of global culture industries—sometimes in an ad hoc, acephalic fashion, sometimes as part of coordinated corporate campaigns aimed at utilizing multiple spaces, places, and situations to reinforce, overlap, and extend the presence and appeal of their products. The expansion of licensing, cross-promotion, in-store product placements, contests, etc., has carried integrated marketing strategies, via multiple media and locations, into nearly all aspects of everyday life. The licensing of spin-off products from major films and television programs is so lucrative (*Jurassic Park* licensing earned the film's producers more than $1 billion) that marketing executives now influence story lines, editorial decisions, camera angles, music scores, and other "creative" aspects of cultural production. The deregulation of television during the Reagan years made possible the notorious "Strawberry Shortcake Strategy," a reference to the first (and by no means the last) children's television character devised by a toy manufacturer to sell merchandise, with story lines derivative from the marketing strategy. When we eat, when we assemble for worship, when we travel, when we go to school—everywhere we go, it seems, we cannot escape the reach of brand names, logos, trademarks, or other corporate imprints on our conscious and subconscious minds.

Place-based marketing had many enthusiasts in the early 1990s, as corporations searched restlessly for new avenues of appeal and reminder: in the pages of books, school classrooms, public bathrooms, movie theaters, mass-transit terminals, doctors' offices, churches. It is not accurate to see place-based advertising as intended to reach people that TV cannot—indeed, TV seems to be able to reach everyone in advanced industrial countries. Rather, place-based strategies seek to amplify the commercial effect, to probe for situations and moods in which another reminder, sales pitch, or visual can help form long-term dispositions useful to firms at another time.

I have already shared numbers about the volume of television watching in advanced capitalist countries. The full magnitude of the culture industry assault on human attention cannot be grasped by attention to television alone, as important as it is. To the three-to-four hours daily of television to which the average American is exposed, one must add:

- 20 or more hours per week of radio (Ekstrom 1992, p. 135);
- 41 pounds of junk mail per adult per year, the opening and sorting of which (according to a *Time* reporter) will consume eight months of a person's lifetime (Smolowe 1990, p. 65; Jacobson and Mazur 1995, p. 123);
- telemarketing that reaches 18 million people per day, courtesy of more than 565,000 companies in an industry that is growing by 30 percent per year (Jacobson and Mazur 1995, p. 127);
- millions of outdoor and billboard advertisements (425,000 on federal highways alone) and countless corporate logos, slogans, and icons worn on clothes by people willing to pay for the privilege of becoming modern-day sandwich boards for corporations (Jacobson and Mazur 1995, p. 133);
- additional mediated encounters via movie theaters, home and personal music equipment, VCRs, and published materials.

Overall, according to one source, a person in the United States encounters approximately 16,000 ads, logos, and the like each day (Savan 1994, p. 1). That we are not fully conscious of the barrage probably preserves our sanity. That we are not fully conscious of the barrage does not mean those messages have no effects on us, as the marketers know so well.

If space is one casualty of the cultural flood, time is another. Consequent to the ceaseless flow and randomness of images, time as an experiential reality seems to change. The past (past information, physical features, clothes, jokes, icons, memories) is constantly surpassed and made obsolete; at the same time, parts of the past are recycled and reassembled in novel combinations.

The flow of images and "output" from global culture industries, especially television, works against memory as habit and as value: humans need not have memory as long as their PCs have sufficient RAM and hard-drive memory. With people in postfordist culture constantly under pressure to keep up with the new, the latest model, the next revolutionary breakthrough, learning about or from the past becomes an obstructionist practice. Forms of learning that require learning from past practitioners, from imitation and gradual internalization of skills and habits, are under attack on nearly all fronts. One result of the denigration of memory and the past is the enfeeblement of imagination and thereby the constraining of the future, the latter limited to being only a continuation, intensification, and expansion of the present. We may therefore be encountering a flood of indefinite duration—not a flood for forty days and forty nights but an eternal flood, a mediated, commercialized, and fully sponsored flood without end.

Implications for Christian Formation

Time Bandits

The first way through which global culture industries undermine practices of Christian formation is the easiest to present. Time spent with television, with recorded music, radio, movies, and the like is almost always time not spent being involved in the sorts of things that form people in practices and affections relevant to the radical demands of the gospel. Entering the world of commodified media, especially television, is so painless, so seductive in terms of form and content, that the hours not spent sleeping or working get absorbed—gradually but in large numbers—into the media whirl. If learning to live, think, and feel through the gospel requires serious learning and apprenticeship for most people, the time-sponge called television leaves no time for such efforts. One would be hard-pressed to learn *any* demanding set of skills or competencies with the amount of time most Catholics in advanced industrial countries devote to their faith tradition. On the other hand, there are few competencies that *cannot* be acquired with 3 to 4 hours per day of time invested—and people in the West use that much time to develop "competence" in television-watching. I am not so stupid to assume that, were TV to disappear tomorrow, people would transfer all their newfound free time to becoming radical disciples of Jesus—indeed, that is the last thing I would expect, given my argument in Chapter 4 about how faith is acquired and transmitted. I do know, however, that so long as people watch such large amounts of television (and work longer hours to pay for the products television has enticed them to buy; see Schor 1991), the gospel will remain a tepid nonessential.

We know how much time people invest with global culture industries. How much, under present circumstances, do they invest in expressing, deepening, or challenging their faith? Recall that behavioral measures of religious involvement (worship attendance, church activities, etc.) tend to be higher in the United States than in other advanced industrial countries (and self-reporting, typical of most U.S. studies, tends to exaggerate involvement). In the United States, according to the most ambitious study of Catholic parish life, only 3 percent of parish-registered Catholics spend 25 hours per month (roughly 6 hours per week) on parish activities outside Mass (Castelli and Gremillion 1987, p. 67); remember that for most American families (Catholic and non-Catholic), television viewing engages them 20 to 25 hours *per week*, or between three and four times as much. The percentages of these high-involvement Catholics would likely be even lower using a larger definition of Catholic membership than that used in this study (described by Castelli and Gremillion 1987, pp. 30–52). Such ratios may produce large numbers of experts on sitcoms and televised sports, but they won't produce saints, martyrs, teachers, or exemplars of the gospel's radical world.

Development of Christian sensibilities via printed media is, if possible, even less promising. In the course of a year, most American Catholics will read no books on contemporary or classical Catholicism, will subscribe to no Catholic periodicals (diocesan or independent, regional or national)— will do nothing, in short, to familiarize themselves with contemporary expression of the faith, diverse theological insights into contemporary problems, or even add to their information base regarding the faith tradition to which they are nominal adherents. The major source for news on Catholicism for American Catholics is the secular media. Under competitive pressures, most news organizations have eliminated specialized beat coverage in labor, religion, minority affairs, and the like, leaving it to nonspecialist reporters to fare as best they can. When the news media cover religion, it is to focus on controversy, scandal, the unusual, or freakish. Such coverage is of no help in nurturing an adult understanding of faith. Most adult Catholics in the United States have been more thoroughly "formed" in their affections and desires by television culture than by the gospel.

The circle, in fact, is nearly complete. Parents raised on television are the primary instructors in faith of their children, who watch even more TV than their parents (the parents reason that TV didn't do *them* any harm, after all). Church leaders themselves are not insulated from the deleterious effects of media monopolization of attention. As one authority in religious education observes:

> People in pastoral ministry often have a difficult time cultivating media literacy in regard to television because this medium so dominates their own lives. Any youth minister or adolescent catechist, for example, under 35, has

had television as a constant companion for his or her entire life. We are just as media saturated as young people. (Sarno 1992, p. 157)

The temptation for church leaders facing such circumstances is apparent: if you can't beat them, join them. With most Catholics attending Mass sporadically at best, not reachable through church newspapers or magazines, not participating in most parish or church activities, how are Catholic leaders to reach "their" people (entertaining the possibility that they are not, and may never have been, "their" people seems too unsettling to most church leaders)?

The answer in many quarters seems to involve adopting wholesale the methods and tactics of global culture industries—via corporate public relations campaigns, advertising agencies, market research, motion pictures, radio/TV production, and more. Although such a posture recognizes the utter inability of existing Catholic channels to reach, much less touch the hearts of, the faithful, the push toward greater use of culture industry vehicles is problematic in the extreme. It presumes the neutrality of culture industry tools, ethically and in terms of effects on communicators, messages, and audiences; such is a profoundly naive and ill-informed view, in my opinion, to which we shall return in the next chapter. Further, such a strategy focuses entirely upon changes external to the church, thereby sidestepping the need to alter its self-assessment and internal operations in a world formed by Disney and McDonald's.

The Invasion of Social Space, the Collapse of Separation

A society inundated with media flow is simultaneously a society under surveillance. People are scrutinized for information on what they buy, watch, eat, enjoy, and loathe and whom they find funny, infuriating, desirable, and worthy of obedience. While we are not yet a totally transparent society, the existing penetration of media flow and surveillance poses serious problems for processes of Christian formation.

In postmodern culture, the notion of unrevealed information, of "secrets," is suspect—all must be available for the inspection of all at all times and in all places. In such a world, there is no room for gradual instruction, for a sequential presentation or unfolding of lessons, habits, or ideas— everything must be present now, corporate information gatherers have the "right" to put any and every aspect of life on display to undifferentiated audiences. In practice this means that all aspects of the Christian tradition, no matter how subtle, paradoxical, or (to use an archaic term) *mysterious*, must be put on display with no regard for people's capacity to understand, appreciate, or appropriate them for themselves.

The catechesis of the early church operated on the assumption that before one could properly appreciate the central mysteries of faith—the Eucharist, losing one's life to gain it, loving one's enemies—one first had to internalize preparatory practices, ideals, and dispositions. The preliminaries, in turn, provided the context within which those mysterious notions were at least partially intelligible on their own terms. Take away those contextualizing and formative preliminaries, and the life and message of Jesus appear as scandal to the Jews and folly to the Greeks (1 Cor 1:22–4).

So it goes in our time, when television, for all its power, is notoriously poor at providing any context or framing outside itself. In fact, television's penetration of all aspects of church life adds to the preposterous images associated with faith; although not all aspects of television's freak-show presentation of religion (speaking in tongues, healings, militant demonstrations, etc.) become more appealing when appropriated by one who has cultivated the capacities for discernment, at least some may appear more intelligible. Put another way, many of the arcane rules and practices of baseball make sense only after one comes to appreciate over time the rhythm, logic, and context of the game. Were television to decontextualize baseball the way it decontextualizes Christianity—presenting hours of nothing but dropped third strikes, heated arguments over what constitutes a balk, and emotional debates for and against the designated-hitter rule—baseball would eventually become unrecognizable (especially if people invested as little time actually playing baseball as they do involved in religiously formative practices).

According to Hobbs, television's decontextualized snippets of information

> help viewers retrieve information about which they already have well-developed schemas for understanding. On the other hand, television's isolated snippets do not help viewers encode information in memory if they don't have sufficient prior knowledge. The 45 seconds on economics or the 35 seconds on elections make it impossible to encode that information if viewers don't have an understanding to begin with. In other words, a few seconds of information is not going to help develop the schemata viewers need to encode this information . . . Watching television news [for example], then, really only helps viewers to reinforce what they already know; it does very little

to make them more sophisticated in these topics other than to provide a few new bits of data. (Hobbs 1991, p. 39)

This concern for prior frameworks is shared by Doris Graber:

When people fail to learn or create appropriate schemas for certain types of news, that news cannot be absorbed. The socialization of average Americans apparently leaves a number of gaps in schema structure. These gaps then make it difficult to focus public attention on some important problems. News about most foreign countries or news about science are examples. Even when such news is presented in simple ways, most of the audience fails to make the effort to absorb it because appropriate schemas did not form part of past socialization. (Hobbs 1991, p. 39, quoting Graber 1984)

Christians can get "well-developed schemas" about Christianity and Jesus only from Christians and the church. When they do not get that, they are more likely to become indistinguishable from the larger media-formed culture in which they live. Joshua Meyrowitz argues that television's erosion of physical and social separation between groups has a homogenizing effect, insofar as particularities are overcome by shared media consumption practices.

Gone, therefore, are many people's "special" behaviors, those that were associated with distinct and isolated interactions. Gone are the great eccentrics, the passionate overpowering loves, the massive unrelenting hates, the dramatic curses and flowery praises. Unbounded joy and unmitigated misery cannot coexist in the same place and time. As situations merge, the hot flush and the icy stare blend into a middle region "cool." (Meyrowitz 1985, p. 311)

As I have argued elsewhere (Budde 1992), the dominant ecclesiology of the Catholic Church in the United States and other advanced industrial countries is "loose" rather than "tight." A loose ecclesiology sees no fundamental incompatibilities between the gospel and the world and therefore sees no need for the Church to maintain any meaningful distance (sociologically or theologically) from the dominant culture. Churches with a loose ecclesiology do not demand or construct space apart, even on a modest scale, from postfordist culture for purposes of Christian formation; consequently they make possible people formed more by the gospel of wealth than the gospel of Jesus, people whose affective rhythms harmo-

nize with the 15-second commercial and jump-cut better than the liturgical calendar.

With little or no social or theological space of their own, without the
capacity to develop Christian affections and practices, the Catholic and
mainline Protestant churches have left people to cobble together their
own "spiritualities" from commercial culture, nationalist ideologies, and
the fragments of Christian and other religious traditions. What emerges
all too often is less than the sum of the parts, usually privileging the ac-
quisitive, feel-good messages of the culture industries and bereft of critical
capacities (except for the sort of self-criticism that can be assuaged by
commercialist interventions). This sort of do-it-yourself spirituality
(called "Sheila-ism" by Bellah and his colleagues, 1985), I argue, is utterly
incapable of radical practices aimed at peace, the option for the poor, or
any demanding exercises in transcending self-interest. There is no Amos
or Jeremiah, no "Woe to you rich" in the canon of Sheila-ism.

Cultural Obstacles to Prayer

No sort of gospel discipleship is possible without a developed capacity for
prayer. Whether studying contemporary or historical exemplars, I have
yet to encounter a church reformer, social radical, martyr, or practitioner
of Christian mercy whose life did not include a spiritual foundation in
which prayer was a crucial aspect. Prayer has taken a number of forms,
moved within many different spiritual traditions, but it has been present
nonetheless.

In this section on how global culture industries subvert processes of
Christian formation—and hence the possibility for a radical gospel discipleship—I want to summarize and expand upon the analysis of Michael
Downey, author of "Hurdles to the Holy: Cultural Obstacles to Prayer"
(1992). His understanding of the nature of prayer and his appraisal of the
contemporary barriers to prayerfulness speak to many of my concerns.

For Downey, although prayer represents "the movement of the human
heart toward an ever more complete awareness of God's presence,"
prayer is not simply or purely a private, individualistic region of practice
or feeling:

Properly understood, the heart is the name for "affectivity," or the affective
dimension of the person, the very openness of the human being to being
touched by another, others, and God . . . As such, it is inclusive of commu-

nal and social realities. To have a heart is to possess the capacity to be in relation. (Downey 1992, p. 46)

Refreshingly, Downey does not ground contemporary barriers to the
development of prayerful capacities in "pluralism." Cultural or social diversity, as he notes, is not uniquely American, Western, or modern—the
Church has made its way in a pluralistic world since its inception. Contrary to the stereotypes, even the High Middle Ages had great cultural variety (p. 49). That our contemporary era presents new obstacles to prayer
is not, therefore, the outworking of cultural pluralism, as if the phenomenon were a new challenge. Of the twelve contemporary impediments to
prayer that Downey identifies, eight directly speak to my concerns regarding television and other culture industries.

The speed and intensity of contemporary life work against the development of prayer. "Whatever our walk of life, we move through our days at
breakneck speed . . . So who has time to pray? We live in an unrelenting
atmosphere of busyness" (p. 51).

That "busyness," idealized by the fast pace of television, makes it difficult "to be still long enough to attend to the presence of God" (p. 52). And
with three to four hours a day devoted to watching television, no wonder
the rest of the day seems compressed and rushed.

> Prayer is not just one more activity, one more thing to do. It is a habit of af-
> fection and behavior, an instinct which, when cultivated and disciplined,
> brings about deeper and fuller recognition of the presence of God "deep
> down things." (Downey 1992, p. 52, quoting Gerard Manley Hopkins)

Culture industries that conquer most nonworking hours of human attention do not leave much time for disciplined cultivation of prayer as a
habitual practice. With the "prime time" of human attention largely pos-
sessed by television, what time and attentiveness that remains for prayer is
residual, marginal, and second-rate.

Downey also identifies the "cacophony and clutter" of our world as serious barriers to prayer.

> Our lives are noisy and cluttered. Traffic, television, loud music that is not
> only harsh and offensive, but dehumanizing, is pumped into restaurants, su-
> permarkets, and even book stores . . . There are just too many sounds and so
> much stuff, things, in our lives. We are filled to the brim with products,
> noises, things. (Downey 1992, p. 52)

The ubiquity of advertising and marketing, and their centrality in post-fordist political economy (as discussed in Chapter Three), generates the "cacophony and clutter" that impede prayerfulness. Downey suggests that persons enticed, seduced, and stimulated incessantly by contemporary advertising/marketing are rendered less fit for authentic spiritual growth.

> The effect of materialism and consumerism is to render us very poor candidates for authentic prayer. For prayer is a movement of the heart, a desire which does not desire this or that object, thing, or sound. Prayer entails the cultivation of a desire which desires only its own increase. The meaning and purpose of praying lies in the waiting. There is nothing to be gotten, no thing to be gained, indeed no sound to be heard, in prayer. (Downey 1992, p. 53)

The flood of noise and busyness, to which culture industries like advertising and television are primary contributors, makes for "congested creativity," according to Downey. We cannot advance toward adaptive and innovative sorts of prayer, cannot find our own voice to or from God, without learning the language of prayer in the context of a teaching community. The apostles asked Jesus, "Teach us to pray," and received the Our Father in reply. In our time, people are too isolated, the ties of church are too thin, to empower the teaching of prayerfulness. People are isolated for many reasons, but the individualizing, privatizing consumption and interaction of media products are among the more important of them. Nor are people served well in this regard by the loose ecclesiology of the Catholic mainstream, in which the parish serves as not much more than an outpatient sacramental dispensary for the majority of persons.

As Downey notes:

> In previous generations, believers were nurtured in cultural contexts ripe with opportunities to be steeped in religious practice. They were taught how to pray from childhood. Just how well or poorly is no doubt arguable. But many today simply do not have a clue about how to pray and, consequently, are diffident about instructing their children to do so. This is not to assign malice. It is simply to say that we are often at a loss when it comes to even the most rudimentary forms of praying. (Downey 1992, pp. 56–7)

Downey suggests that the rote memorization of simple prayers has been set aside, with nothing to replace it—depriving large numbers of Christians of another source of basic familiarity with the biblical story, scriptural allusions, and the process of prayer. "Many are simply at a loss, not just for words, but for a single clue regarding how to cultivate the intuition for God's abiding presence" (p. 57).

The obsession with speed, instantaneousness, and easy gratification characteristic of electronic media corrupts people's capacities to pray, according to Downey.

> Helpful though all this [fax, satellite, telephone, etc.] may be, these modes of quick communication may be misleading and indeed detrimental if we expect praying to be anything like this. In prayer, there is no instant contact. We do not get quick information. The answers to our questions and meager conundrums are not met with ready reply, if indeed a reply is forthcoming at all. (Downey 1992, p. 54)

Like other commentators, Downey finds contemporary culture industries infused with narcissism and self-glorification:

> We are finite, and so must gradually but certainly move through stages of diminishment, frailty, dying, and death. This is what is to be faced in prayer. How are we to travel this path in serenity and poised confidence when we are glutted with information on billboards and TV which, while seducing us into the cult of youth and beauty, signals this denial of our contingency, woundedness, vulnerability, and frailty? (Downey 1992, p. 55)

Overall, many of Downey's cultural obstacles to prayer are rooted in or strengthened by the formal properties of culture industries discussed in earlier chapters. I am persuaded by his appraisal of the role of media content, especially regarding the conflict between consumerist dispositions and the capacity for prayer. He also argues convincingly that it is not pluralism but more specific phenomena—many rooted in the influence of global culture industries—that present new impediments to prayer. And without learning skills and habits of prayer (broadly understood), no serious formation of Christian practices and affections can occur.

Symbolic Predators

Learning to become a Christian has always involved more than learning doctrine. Especially (but not exclusively) in the Catholic tradition, it has also involved learning how to respond to sacred symbols of the faith, how to use holy symbols as aids in prayer and meditation, and how to learn the stories, roles, and exemplars of faith through imagery, symbol, and sacrament. For Christian formation to work best, there must be some coherence to the sacred symbols employed by the Church in any given era (which does not preclude gradual change in the meaning of those symbols over time). While Christian formation does not require the non-Christian world to participate in the symbolic universe of Christians, the process is impeded when outside forces threaten to overwhelm, undermine, or drown out the communicative functions of religious symbols and images.

In recent decades, global culture industries like television and advertising have begun to exploit religious imagery in ever more overt, crass, and trivial ways. They have come to operate as "symbolic predators," cultural parasites seeking to profit from repositories of meaning and socialization they did not create and which they weaken by their encroachment. Let me be more specific, this time with reference to television advertising, an example that brings together consideration of the two culture industries we have examined thus far.

One consequence of the accommodationist orientation and practice of mainline religious traditions in the United States (e.g., Herberg 1955; Cuddihy 1978; Budde 1992) is a broad-but-not-deep socialization of members into religious traditions, stories, and motifs. This should not be confused with any sort of religious proficiency or deep understanding (for example, although the population of the United States is still largely Christian, at least nominally, levels of basic religious ignorance are strikingly high). In fact, the failure of religious communities to instill more than a surface familiarity with biblical and religious symbols, stories, and images makes their corporate hijacking simultaneously easier and noncontroversial (because those symbols, stories, and images are both vaguely familiar and not especially vital to most people). The religious communities as a group have been unable or unwilling to protect their sacred stories and symbols from this exploitation. Indeed, all too often, they seem not to recognize the pillaging in process.

This submerged, incomplete fluency in matters religious provides points of reference to be exploited by advertisers as they associate products with evocative images, motifs, and narratives in nonlogical, varied ways. As Gregor Goethals notes, the appropriation of religiosity is most pronounced in commercial sales pitches. "The most condensed format of the conversionist motif [in American culture] is the TV commercial, which has become essential to both network and religious broadcasting.

Embedded in its structure are sentiments from our religious and political heritage: salvation and choice" (Goethals 1990, p. 116).

But the appropriation of religious resources is not always overt or crass. Religious symbols are still too "hot" to manipulate with abandon—we won't see Jesus on the cross used to pitch deodorant anytime soon—but when appropriately subdued, buried, and nonobvious, many of the classic narratives of Judaism and Christianity (e.g., Exodus, miracles, resurrection) act effectively as deep structures in commercial messages.

Turning to contemporary U.S. television ads and their expropriation of religiosity, consider the following examples:

- Oil of Olay asks us to "believe in" its promise of youth and beauty, a demand calling for a response of faith. Oil of Olay in turn "keeps its promise" to users—a covenant between the (re)Creator of life and beauty and us, the worshipping faithful.
- Spirit soap (note the name) reveals the secret to its ability to bestow vitality and a healthy glow—namely, a classic Trinitarian synthesis of three soaps in one, a unity of essence that encompasses a plurality/diversity of personal needs.
- Coca-Cola's world commercials, airing during the 1992 Summer Olympic games, construct a universal brotherhood of corporate consumption, fulfilling the Great Commission (Mt 28:19-20) in ways Matthew never imagined. Coke gathers together all the nations of the world, enemies and friends, within the embrace of its red and white logo, its hymnodic jingle, and the universal, transcendent appeal of its product.
- AT&T's world calling commercial focuses on miraculous transformations, with a row of little girls in First Communion dresses metamorphosed into a flame-breathing dragon character straight from a Chinatown New Year's gala, with nuns in full habit transfigured and transported half a world away. Throughout, one gets transfiguration and (thanks to AT&T) the revelation that everyone in the whole world is now our neighbor and only a phone call away.
- Oxy-10 acne cream, in its campaign to "Oxy-cute" pimples, features young boys with pimples hiding in the shadows, away from the light—they are social lepers, not unlike those forced into seclusion in New Testament accounts. For these twentieth-century pariahs, however, healing comes not from the touch of Jesus but from a bottled cream. Once healed and restored to social respectability,

one young boy emerges, smiling and healthy, into the light, thanks to Jesus-as-acne-cream.

- IBM, in a recent campaign, employs nuns in full habit swapping techno-nerd insights (in a foreign language) while strolling through their European-style cloister. Even the most isolated communities know of IBM (even those not known as world communicators) and have come to appreciate the advantages of the new OS/2 Warp system (with full Internet connectivity, no less).
- MCI employed the priest-accountant of a religious community to tell of the nearly miraculous savings enjoyed when the community switched long-distance companies. The trustworthiness of the priests and priests-in-training, in turn, is supposed to carry over to the trust that we can comfortably invest in MCI (as have these holy people).
- Timex, seeking (like other firms) to boost its image of trustworthiness, contrasts the reputation of advertising executives with that of a priest, in an ironic, audience-flattering pitch that we as audience are savvy enough to understand.
- Carnation Hot Chocolate presents two small children in winter clothes waiting in vain for snowfall and winter fun. They are found, forlorn and powerless, by an old man with white hair and white beard. This Santa Claus/God the Father figure takes pity on them and brings them inside for the magic taste of Carnation Hot Chocolate. This beverage does more than warm and refresh—like Jesus and other divine figures, Carnation Hot Chocolate controls the forces of nature: it begins to snow.
- In one African-American family, a young man returns home from a job interview with Dow, the chemical conglomerate. This young man has been chosen, called to an important job—converting energy consumption away from environmentally destructive sources. "Sounds like an important job," says the wizened father. But it's so far away, complain other family members. Ultimately, the son is sent forth by the father to show what the younger can do for the world, to accept his vocation of worldwide environmental salvation. To enable the son's work to reach more widely, he is sent to Dow, a community of disciples/believers whose vocation is one of serving and redeeming the fallen/polluted environment. No mention is made of napalm, Agent Orange, or other Dow contributions to the natural environment.

- A spot for Nestlé Cappuccino describes the product as embodying a "small miracle," underscored by a shot of a monk in silhouette lifting a scoop of coffee beans. Cappuccino, as a beverage named after the Capuchin community of monks—and as reinforced by the visuals here—carries the qualities of peace and serenity associated with meditative, contemplative lifestyles.
- In perhaps the most succinct statement of materialist theology, a current Mercedes-Benz spot promises a litany of blessings and ends with the slogan "Sacrifice nothing."

Conclusion

As is apparent by now, for me Christian formation—becoming people who "seek first the Kingdom of God," who become a Church capable of living (however imperfectly) the alternative reality proposed by Jesus—presupposes the necessity and virtue of distinctiveness. Christians are not supposed to be like "everyone else," and "being a Christian" is a strenuous undertaking not to be watered down in order to bring everyone in.

Difference, diversity, and identity are among the celebrated aspects of postmodern culture. Gender, race, ethnicity, and region have re-emerged as bases for collective action, ideology, and politics in a world in which modern, "universal" claimants of value, normativity, and authority have been weakened, if not fatally wounded.

Beneath the dizzying array of cultural choices, however, remains the oligopolistic substratum of the global culture industries. For all the surface diversity—Lebanese cooking shows and Australian football and Balinese dance and Borscht Belt comedians and navel-pierced singers and purple dinosaurs and round-the-clock news snippets—the dominant culture industries have concentrated decisions in amazingly few centers: Disney/ABC, Sony, Bertlesman, Time-Warner, GE/NBC, and the like. And although hundreds of television channels promise more choices in viewing options (a debatable premise on several levels), what they surely will deliver are more hours spent viewing television. This is true for the United States, where the saturation levels remain undefined, but it is even more true for those parts of the world in which global culture industries (especially television) anticipate their greatest growth. Industry analysts expect to add 100 million new television sets (attached to cable and/or satellite programming) in India and China within the next five years;

China is estimated to have a potential television market of 900 million people (Schodolski and Dretzka 1995, sec. 1, p. 1).

The amount of time invested by Christians in the enterprises of global culture industries (in advanced industrial countries and, increasingly, in other parts of the world), the seriousness with which these are pursued, and the surrender of Christians to the influences of these enterprises—all of these make authentic Christian formation increasingly difficult in ways not known to earlier generations. The "orchestrators of attention" (Warren 1992, p. 3) benefit from techniques that may be more effectively distracting than the medieval festivals, the excesses of Corinth, or devotees of Canaanite cults.

To the extent that Catholics and other Christians have managed to resist the leveling and homogenizing effects of heavy television immersion (see for example Morgan 1984, on such effects), it is due largely to the persistence of socialization structures and habits developed in the times before media inundation. These socialization structures and processes, when deep and effective, offered the potential for critical reception of mediated flow, a chance (albeit limited) to be the "active audience" so celebrated by many cultural studies scholars. The capacity of audiences to construct "critical readings," or "subversive interpretations," of media texts, it seems to me, presupposes the presence and vitality of nonmedia ways of "forming" persons into an alternative story. And it is precisely these other ways of "forming" people that are withering in the cultural environment of postfordist capitalism.

"Making Christians" is a demanding process under the best of conditions—since the beginning, many interested persons have walked away when confronted with the radical demands of the gospel (Lk 18:18–23). In our day, after centuries of understating the demands of the Christian life, church leaders confront a situation in which the thin formation offered to the majority of Catholics is so easily overwhelmed by the global culture industries that have captured and monopolized the attention of nearly everyone in advanced industrial countries. Christians spend thousands of hours a year interacting with complex systems that, in ways not fully understood, impact our desires, temperament, predispositions, and sense of normality. Far from being distinctive in themselves, Christians see their once-distinctive stories and symbols deployed against them in efforts to make them buy, desire, and dream like everyone else. Liberal reform notions to the contrary, the main "problem" with global culture industries is not "bad" content and will not be addressed with "better" content. The church does not gain if the 20 to 30 hours of TV viewing each week changes from cops and sleaze to socially uplifting messages—it wouldn't gain from 20 to 30 hours of TV viewing of religious programming, for that matter. With so many hours of human existence in the thrall of commercial culture industries, with human attention surrounded by barkers and enticers and noisemakers, the quiet but single-minded call to the gospel cannot be heard.

Winning back members of the Body of Christ will not be done by imitating the techniques of the culture industries. Those who can be ransomed will be drawn to a radically reformed and revitalized vision of the church and its role in Jesus' mission—or they will not be ransomed at all.

6

Church Barriers to Understanding Global Culture Industries

One looks in vain for a systematic treatment of global culture industries in the official pronouncements of the Vatican Council, popes, or Curial offices. Although individual episcopal conferences or dioceses deal with culture industries in more or less ad hoc fashion, consideration of culture industries as a group is largely absent from the highest levels of church leadership.

Having said that, it remains true that the *component* aspects of global culture industries have been discussed—most of it has focused on mass media, the morality of media content, and the usefulness of electronic media for the work of the Church. Others have summarized the main statements from Catholic leaders, including World Communications Day statements, pronouncements on mass media, television, and the like (e.g., Rossi and Soukup 1993; Granfield 1994), and there is no need to duplicate their efforts.

The need does exist, however, to point to—and beyond—the barriers to understanding the global culture industries that are constructed by many official Church statements to date. Not all of these apply equally to every bishop, administrator, or policymaker, but they are in sufficiently wide circulation (or carry sufficient influence) to warrant attention. To the extent that these barriers remain unrecognized or underappreciated, so too will one's grasp of the significance of culture industries for the life of the Church remain inadequate or incomplete. These conceptual inadequacies, in turn, inform many of the pastoral practices in religious education and lay formation that are not up to the task of forming Christian disciples in postfordist cultures.

Barrier I: Sacramental Liberalism,
the Interpretive Key

A common interpretive thread pervades the primary Vatican II document on mass media (*Inter Mirifica* 1963), subsequent documents by the Pontifical Commission for Social Communication (*Communio et Progressio* 1971), and the annual World Communications Day messages by the popes. Expressed variously in these documents, the benchmark assumption is something we might call sacramental liberalism—the notion that since all of Creation is made by God and judged good by God (Gn 1:31), all natural and human projects can in principle be revelatory of God and useful for divine purposes. Sacramental liberalism stands against any sort of dualism—Manichaeism comes to mind—that denigrates the material world or equates "the world" with utter sinfulness and evil. All aspects of material creation or human initiative can be used for good or bad purposes (and can be judged based on those uses), but a priori none can be condemned completely as incompatible with the Christian vision. This is an assumption highly prized in Catholic theological circles, one held proudly as an alternative to some more pessimistic Protestant views that come dangerously close to denying the goodness of the created order.

With reference to mass media, sacramental liberalism is nowhere better expressed than in recent Vatican documents. The most recent, *Aetatis Novae* (1991), has been described by several analysts to be a more measured, less optimistic document than *Inter Mirifica* (1963) or *Communio et Progressio* (1971). This latest document is more aware of the problems generated or exacerbated by mass media—social isolation, deformed portrayals of family, sexuality, and religion, advertiser-fueled consumerism, and more (e.g., Secs. 5, 7). Despite these manifest problems, the Pontifical Council affirms the judgment of *Communio et Progressio* that the Church "sees these media as 'gifts of God,' which in accordance with his providential design unite men in brotherhood and so help them to cooperate with his plan for their salvation" (*Communio et Progressio*, Sec. 2, quoted in *Aetatis Novae*, Sec. 22). This more "critical" appraisal of media culture can nevertheless affirm a strong (and naive) teleology in which a whole litany of typical for-profit media practices are

> contrary to the principal purposes and indeed to the very nature of the media, whose proper and essential social role consists in contributing to the realization of the human right to information, promoting justice in the pursuit

of the common good, and assisting individuals, groups, and peoples in their search for truth. (*Aetatis Novae,* Sec. 14)

I confess to some anxiety and frustration as a Catholic scholar struggling with many contemporary uses of "sacramentality" in social ethics and theological discourse. It is a basic category of Catholic Christian thought, to which one can hardly object at a certain general level (the created order cannot be intrinsically evil or irredeemable, since it both sustains life and is included in the redemptive promises of God). On the other hand, the "sacramentality" of creation and human action is bandied about so casually and unreflectively in Catholic circles that critical appraisal—let alone critical judgment—is disqualified from the outset. At times, the reality and pervasiveness of sin seem overlooked entirely.

To criticize the Church's leadership for misunderstanding the importance and workings of global culture industries because of an excessive attachment to sacramental liberalism forces one to walk a fine line. What can and must be said is that sacramental liberalism falls short as a guide to theologically informed critique for several reasons, not least because it commits several sorts of category errors while ignoring questions of systematic and interactive relations in human societies.

Recall that I mentioned already that one mostly searches in vain for Church leaders' appraisals on global culture industries as industries—as a mix of economics, regulatory frameworks, technology, and cultural production. Here lies a clue to one shortcoming in sacramental liberalism— its highly reductive tendencies. Its proponents prefer to downplay analyses of systems and interactions in favor of decontextualized appraisals of parts and components. It would be as if one studied first-strike nuclear weapons without regard for nationalism, patterns and objectives of political domination, and the loss of human and nonhuman life attendant to their use. Instead, by analyzing such weapons as aggregations of electrical engineering, high energy physics, and metallurgy (all of which, taken singly, make contributions to human betterment), even offensive nuclear weapons can be seen as evocative of God's good creation.

This is not how Church leaders and documents have chosen to analyze the theological and pastoral implications of nuclear weapons. But in their treatment of culture industries, one does see this excessive privileging of "parts"—specific technologies, isolated examples of novel uses, and so on—to the neglect of careful analyses of systems and structures. This represents a conceptual levels-of-analysis error: because the components can be "sacramental" in some fashion, their positioning and regularized interactions in *systems* must be similarly sacramental. While major Church statements on mass media do express token concern for macro-level, structural considerations (*Aetatis Novae*, Secs. 5, 13), these are outweighed theologically and analytically by the overriding privileging of the good to be had via the components.

The second shortcoming of such statements flows from the reductionism of the first. Joined to the levels-of-analysis confusion typical of major Vatican statements is an excessive privileging of "agency" over "structure" in appraising mass media in our day. Documents such as *Communio et Progressio* and *Aetatis Novae* imply that undesirable uses and consequences of media (fixation on sensationalism, consumerism, superficiality) are mostly caused by individual decisionmakers whose consciences haven't been formed by Catholic (or other suitably ethical) social norms. This can be remedied, or at least rectified substantially, by chaplaincy-type efforts from the Church to media personnel ("good" uses can be encouraged via prizes, awards, and the like as well) (see *Aetatis Novae*, Sec. 24).

That the structural relations (of finance, for example) that shape the decision parameters of media personnel are not totalizing in their effects seems to be grounds for denying, in these analyses, that structural relations privilege *any* tendencies, predispositions, or generally operant probabilities with regard to media. It is as if, to borrow from Postman (1985), one pointed to the theoretical possibility of mimes performing on radio to argue against the notion that radio is well-suited for sound broadcasting and that sound broadcasting will likely prove more commonplace than mime contests. One can imagine it, in other words, but how likely—given all the pressures, affinities, interests being served—is it? Much of the Vatican's analysis of media is analogous—the documents can conjure a variety of pro-social and pro-Christian uses of mass media, but are they any more likely than radio coverage of mime events? Individual decisionmakers, in other words, may be highly constrained in their autonomy, a point considered insufficiently or not at all in the documents discussed here.

The political economy sections of Chapters 2 and 3 remind us that although the structural position of global culture industries in postfordist capitalism is not fully determinative of every micro-level decision, it does make some outcomes and decisions far more likely or regular than others. By identifying "good" uses and possibilities in the for-profit media world, regardless of how likely or prevalent such may be now or in the future,

Vatican statements dodge all the hard questions that attach to culture industries as structures within capitalism.

Barrier II: The Evangelization Fixation

The highest leaders in the church were and still mostly are fixated on the seemingly unlimited benefits that mass media promise regarding evangelization efforts. Despite its resistance to other aspects of modernity, the Church has embraced each new communications innovation as a providential aid in fulfilling the Great Commission (Matt 28:19–20). So strong is this belief that the global culture industries and the worlds their tools have made will remain mostly insulated from any institutional Catholic critique of a rigorous sort; for to do so might imply that under given circumstances the Church ought *not* embrace the tools, techniques, and social arrangements attendant to collaboration with global culture industries. That is a policy decreed unacceptable from the outset.

Many Vatican and papal pronouncements on mass media, communications, and the like feel compelled to quote approvingly Paul VI's sweeping statement from *Evangelii Nuntiandi*:

> When [the mass media] are put at the service of the Gospel, they are capable of increasing almost indefinitely the area in which the Word of God is heard, they enable the Good News to reach millions of people. *The Church would feel guilty before the Lord if she did not utilize these powerful means that human skill is daily rendering more perfect.* It is through them that she proclaims "from the housetops," the message of which she is the depository. In them she finds a modern and effective version of the pulpit. Thanks to them she succeeds in speaking to the multitudes. (*Evangelii Nuntiandi 1975*, Sec. 45; emphasis added)

In calling for media-use training for all priests, religious, and bishops, Archbishop John Foley, President of the Pontifical Council for Social Communications, argues that the mass media are the "primary means" to "proclaim [Jesus'] Good News from the housetops and to all nations" (1994, p. 6). The U.S. Catholic bishops, in turn, "rejoice in the unparalleled pastoral opportunities we have to share the light of the Gospel with all people," as a result of advances in mass media and communications (USCC 1986, p. 5).

While these and many other Church documents seem to imply that the Church can utilize mass media however it pleases, on other occasions Church leaders acknowledge something critical: the audiences for mass-mediated evangelization have entrenched, strongly held expectations regarding the media products they will accept. The authors of *Communio et Progressio* conceded:

> People today have grown so used to the entertaining style and skillful presentation of communications by the media that they are intolerant of what is obviously inferior in any public presentation. The same applies if this be a religious occasion, such as, for example, a liturgical ceremony, a sermon, or instruction in the faith.
>
> In order to make the teaching of Christianity more interesting and effective, the media should be used as much as possible. Every effort should be made to use the most appropriate technique and style in fitting a communication to its medium. (*Communio et Progressio*, Secs. 130, 131)

Ironically, although many Church documents analyze the component parts of culture industries in a reductive fashion, when discussion turns to evangelization via mass media those same authors become acutely aware of cultural ecology and the formative impact of media consumption. In the former circumstances, media can be utilized in nearly any way one chooses; in the latter, the real range of choice is highly constrained by the prior effects of culture industries on audience expectations, competence, and toleration. For the Church to use the tools of for-profit culture industries to "evangelize cultures" (a favorite phrase of John Paul II, among others), it must abide by the formulae (e.g., entertainment) and formal qualities (fast-paced, high-intensity, decontextualized) privileged by those industries and disseminated to billions of people each day.

One can't help but wonder: Given that most people in the world are being formed and taught by commercial media in their understanding of what constitutes "good" television (or cinema, advertising, or whatever), how far are Church leaders willing to go in conforming to the norms of the culture industries? Will the Church train its personnel in manipulative, psychographic-style research, and seductive "associative advertising" techniques as part of the media training it envisions in *Aetatis Novae* (Sec. 18)? Will Catholic media campaigns become indistinguishable from U.S. television evangelists, who are far ahead in adapting the gospel to the formats of commercial media?

Imagine the maximal case: Having sold everything salable in the Catholic world, having received hundreds of billions of dollars from Catholic benefactors, the Pope buys CBS from Westinghouse, NBC from General Electric, Fox from Rupert Murdoch, and ABC from Disney (what the heck—let him buy the Mouse too). Let the Pope buy Time-Warner, Bertelsmann, Sony, and J. Walter Thompson. Then what? Can the Great Commission finally be fulfilled, now that the tools are in pious hands? What will change—indeed, what *can* change—under the circumstances? If these high-tech media institutions are not to decay into worthlessness, they will need regular infusions of money—lots of it—to keep spinning out the sounds and sights. Will Church ownership reduce the constraints of finance, advertising, and the entertainment imperative? Or will, as seems more likely, the Church use the institutions as money pumps that extract revenue from consumers and audiences in order to keep the "evangelization industries" functioning? Even if the boosters of media-as-evangelizers get everything they want, what will they have? Not much worth having, I suspect, unless one fully and finally redefines the Christian gospel as just another commodity to be sold using any and all means (including coercive ones).

I have seen no convincing evidence to support the contention that by playing the culture industries' game the processes of evangelization, religious education, or catechesis are advanced. These activities may be served more adequately by small-scale, limited media (VCRs, audio tapes, etc.), although (as I will discuss in the next chapter) only under certain and rather restricted circumstances.

I have a hard time explaining the tenacity with which Church leaders hold out hope for using the culture industries to evangelize the world (thus exempting those industries from more critical scrutiny), except with reference to the potential for mass media to compensate for the weaknesses attendant to a loose, minimalist ecclesiology. Even though mass media such as television, advertising, public relations, and the like may not really work to make the gospel a living reality in the world, perhaps they help the Church in other, less visible, ways.

Not enough priests? No problem—many of the educative and community-building functions of clergy can be taken over by polished, professional media figures (removing the need, incidentally, to consider women in the ordained ministry). Parishes too impersonal and lifeless? No problem—take a warmer, affirming gospel directly to the cozy intimacy of the home, where people are used to getting media reassurances that they are special and loved. Unresponsive, uninvolved church members? No problem—reaching people via media makes fewer demands on them except for financial support to keep the electronic outreach moving forward (just like the TV preachers or PBS pledge nights with which they're already familiar).

Kids don't know anything about the Christian tradition? No problem—get a few "Christian rock" videos in heavy rotation between the usual fare on MTV, so kids can become committed Christians in the isolated privacy of their own rooms. Maybe we can tie in some merchandising opportunities for saints' clothing, caps, action figures, and fast-food franchises at the same time—imagine the Last Supper as a McDonald's Happy Meal, presided over by Ronald McDonald and attended by Mayor McCheese and friends.

One could continue listing the sorts of ecclesial weaknesses for which electronic media can be seen as the solution. What becomes apparent—as both cause and consequence of the generally uncritical enthusiasm for global culture industries—is a final barrier to thinking more clearly about the matters at hand.

Barrier III: Is the Church Becoming a "Culture Industry"?

Ultimately, the Church's leaders may be incapable of recognizing the threats to Christian practice and life because they are remaking the Church in the image and likeness of the global culture industries. The process is far from complete, and may (with considerable effort and redirection) be halted, but the trends can be discerned. As they begin adopting the techniques, worldviews, and criteria of advertising/marketing and mass commercial media, Church leaders make it more likely that whatever elements of gospel nonconformity and radical discipleship yet endure will be buried beneath the data of focus groups, Q-scores, psychographic profiles, and multimedia campaigns.

As with Foucault's power/knowledge ideas, no conspiracy or cabal within the Church "directs" or orchestrates such a transformation of the Church and its mission. Given the Church's commitment to a minimalist ecclesiology, and given the changed cultural ecology within which it works in many parts of the world, it is not surprising to see Church leaders at many levels imitating the processes of the marketing industry. Nor am I saying that the incorporation of a marketing ethos is complete—

many Church leaders, for example, complain that inadequate financing is slowing their efforts to utilize fully the power of media, advertising, and related industries. And contrary to the cultured despisers of Christianity, who see nothing new in the Church adopting the best tools with which to bamboozle the gullible, I believe there *are* qualitative differences between the past and the emerging present.

I suggest that three interrelated phenomena put the Church on the path of transformation into something it should not become, something like a commercial culture industry.

The Church as Retailer

Although recent studies of materialism and religion shed light on the anthropological significance of religiously sanctioned goods (R. L. Moore 1994; McDaniel 1995), something new is afoot these days. Like Disney and Time-Warner, the Catholic Church is establishing formal licensing arrangements to generate income for Church activities. Product tie-ins, joint promotions, licensing arrangements—though not yet large compared with commercial firms—are becoming more frequent and widely pursued by Catholic leaders.

Much of this merchandising is tied in with the tours and appearances of the most marketable Catholic personality of the day, Pope John Paul II. In 1993, Catholic leaders (in what is believed to be the first formal venture of this kind) contracted with Famous Artists Merchandising Exchange to coordinate licensing of more than 100 products tied to the Pope's appearance at World Youth Day in Denver. The Dayton, Ohio, firm, whose past clients include the Rolling Stones, Paul McCartney, Paul Simon, and the Toronto Blue Jays, envisioned merchandising revenue large enough to cover a full 20 percent of the Church's World Youth Day costs (Janofsky 1993, p. D-1).

Alas, this initial venture ended unhappily. The U.S. bishops sued Famous Artists over $850,000 in unpaid royalties due the Church. Famous Artists, in turn, countersued World Youth Day, Inc. (the bishops' spin-off organization charged with event coordination) with allegations of breach of contract and fraudulent misrepresentation (Religious News Service 1994, Sec. 2, p. 9). In particular, Famous Artists claimed that because some Church groups allowed liberal use of the papal insignia, colors, and images, the "value" of items produced by Famous Artists' licensees was reduced.

The moral of the story, as learned by the Archdiocese of Newark, is to cut out the middleman and conduct merchandising and licensing on one's own. This is what the Archdiocese did in conjunction with the Pope's stopover Mass at Giant Stadium on October 21, 1994. Hoping to avoid the sort of problems that led the U.S. bishops and Famous Artists to court, the Archdiocese ran a major merchandising/licensing program from its central purchasing office. According to a spokesman, the marketing of the Pope was inevitable. "So why not us?" he insisted (Goldman 1994, p. 8).

More recently, and much more ambitiously, the Vatican has authorized merchandise "inspired" by the Vatican Library's collection of more than one million books, 100,000 prints and drawings, and other holdings. Having taken on a corporate partner for the venture, spokespersons estimate initial licensing revenue to the Vatican of $5 million per year for the first 5 years, rising to $10 to $20 million per year for the following 15 years (Kirk 1995, p. 45).

Further, the Vatican has entered a partnership with IBM in order to digitize the entire holdings of the Vatican Library. IBM is spending $1 million a year to scan 20,000 images in the multiyear project; the resulting information will become part of the IBM Digital Library, which will combine the Vatican holdings with those of other major institutional archives. While the intent of the venture, according to Vatican and IBM public relations releases, is to increase access to the Vatican's holdings beyond the 2,000 scholars who visit annually, the terms of such access were not addressed in news accounts (see Tagliabue 1995, p. A-5; Lohr 1995, p. D-3). Would the Vatican collection be free to all interested parties (via the Internet, for example)? Or would it be available only on a pay-per-view Internet arrangement, or via CDs sold by IBM or another software/content provider? While IBM gains public relations points by providing access to the digitized Vatican library, both IBM and the Vatican stand to reap potentially large financial returns by selling the processed patrimony of the Church.

The Disney company is not content simply to license products based on old characters and cultural products (e.g., Snow White, Mickey Mouse); instead, it constantly produces new cultural (and copyrighted) "product" that may be exploited across a variety of media. The Vatican, likewise, is moving from reliance on old cultural artifacts to producing (and selling) new religious/cultural goods. In the person of John Paul II, the Church has a worldwide media personality with high visibility and popularity ratings in multiple markets.

And so, like Colin Powell and Newt Gingrich, John Paul II has entered the ranks of big-advance authors in the employ of global publishers. Based on sales of the new Catholic Catechism (1.6 million copies worldwide), Alfred A. Knopf, Inc. (now a division of Random House) in 1994 paid a $9 million advance for the rights to *Crossing the Threshold of Hope*, a collection of spiritual and philosophical musings by the pontiff.

The worldwide promotional push involved simultaneous releases in 21 languages and 35 countries, with extensive public relations campaigns in major cities coordinated by the Italian publisher Arnaldo Mondadori Editore, which acquired the worldwide rights to *Crossing the Threshold of Hope*. Interestingly, Italian media mogul Silvio Berlusconi (an ex-prime minister indicted on corruption charges) retains a 47 percent stake in Mondadori after selling part of his stake to raise cash earlier in 1994. Sources project worldwide grosses from *Crossing the Threshold of Hope* to be between $100 and $200 million (Tagliabue 1994, p. A-5).

While *Crossing the Threshold of Hope* is not John Paul's first published book, it does represent a new level of commercial partnership and promotion between the Vatican and global media concerns. Having graduated into the ranks of the nonfiction big time (due primarily to the all-out promotional efforts of Random House) with *Crossing the Threshold of Hope*, it is unlikely that future popes or the Vatican will be willing to bite the hand that feeds the royal coffers. And to the extent that Vatican administrators (like their culture industry counterparts) measure success in terms of "units" sold, the advantages of utilizing the culture industries' ways are manifest: *Love and Responsibility*, published in English by tiny Farrar, Strauss, and Giroux (for a $25,000 fee), sold between 15,000 and 20,000 copies. Harper San Francisco's 1992 collection of homilies and speeches to U.S. Catholics sold "way under 5,000" copies, due to a lack of promotion; that house's most successful papal book, *Things of the Spirit*, sold only 12,000 copies (Lyall 1994, p. C-11).

Having tasted success the culture industries' way, the Pope has diversified into other media. The most recent (1996) offering is a multimedia package (video, compact disc) of the Pope praying the rosary. The promotional strategy includes—for the first time, perhaps—using the Pope himself as the pitchman in television ads, supported by radio and print advertising. While the TV ads are promised to be "tasteful" and "understated" (using old footage of John Paul walking in the outdoors), the notion of the Pope as yet another media huckster and product endorser begs for parody, if nothing else.

The papal rosary project, like *Crossing the Threshold of Hope,* involves a multinational, multilingual release. Royalties are dedicated to the support of Vatican Radio and its $15 million per year budget. Curiously, Vatican sources say, the rosary project is seen as an alternative to allowing advertising on Vatican Radio. It is hard to understand the resistance to advertising on Vatican Radio as anything other than outdated sentiment, however. Having shown the willingness to put the Vicar of Christ out front as pitchman, what could be objectionable to "tasteful," "understated" ads for McDonald's, EuroDisney, or Smith and Wesson on Vatican Radio?

It remains to be seen whether this sort of promotion represents an aberration, a one-time event. Given the need for Vatican Radio and other Church programs to generate revenue, and given the apparently increased (and widely diffused) enthusiasm among Church leaders for advertising and marketing, such seems increasingly implausible.

"Step Right Up!" Hyping the Gospel, Growing the Church

> *If he were here today, St. Paul would be Madison Avenue.*
> **—Bernard Cardinal Law of Boston**

Give him credit for clarity, if not insight. In one line that echoes of liberal Protestant manuals from the early twentieth century, Cardinal Law captures everything wrong about much of the Church's understanding of itself, its mission, and the culture industries that are reshaping our environment. For my part, I have problems envisioning many advertising executives being imprisoned and tortured for the sake of an "account." Nor can I see—except in a Monty Python sketch—St. Paul hawking the gospel with bimbo models, promises of health and wealth, and intimations of enhanced sexual satisfaction. The church in Corinth may have been willing to try such promotional methods, but Paul probably would not have liked it much.

While not all Church leaders are as openly enthusiastic about Madison Avenue in the Church, the role of professional advertising/marketing agencies seems on the rise across a range of Church activities. This sort of thing is a far cry from block-print ads on the back of parish bulletins, a new Pontiac donated to a church raffle, or other small-scale, low-tech practices that almost seem quaint by comparison.

They are a world away, for example, from the United States Catholic Conference's $5 million contract with Hill and Knowlton (among the largest, and most notorious, public relations firms in the world); using the latest in market research techniques and advertising strategy, the firm attempted to boost the sagging fortunes of the bishops' anti-abortion efforts.

The amateurish efforts of the past are also a world away from Saatchi & Saatchi's $4 million per year contract with the Italian Catholic Church, which hoped to entice taxpayers to designate the Church as their choice for tax-supported charity (Wentz 1990, p. 8). The Church switched its account to another division of a transnational ad agency a few years later, after having heard pitches from other firms bidding for the account (which had grown to $7 million per year by then; see *Advertising Age* 1992a,b). Dioceses and religious congregations now utilize corporate ad agencies to invite disaffected Catholics back to the Church, to encourage priestly and religious vocations, and improve and modernize the image of the Church. Not all of them have yet moved in step with the "Big 5" churches in Britain (the Church of England, the Roman Catholic Church, and the Methodist, Baptist, and United Reformed Churches) that decided the Church's image is easier to boost if one deliberately omits all cruciform images from advertising—even (or especially) at Easter (ENI 1995b). It may be only a matter of time, however.

For their part, corporate ad agencies are eager to work with churches; marketing professors have noted with interest that "the clergy seems to be more open to advertising than the general public." Churches, in the eyes of ad execs, represent "viable potential clients for advertising services," among the largest groups in the underserved (by ad agencies, anyway) nonprofit sector (McDaniel 1986, p. 28). Church and nonprofit clients also represent opportunities for ad firms to boost their good-neighbor credentials, win awards, and make contacts useful for attracting for-profit accounts (Stern 1986, pp. 42–4).

Although reliable figures on Church advertising are nonexistent, there are several reasons to suggest that the Catholic Church in many advanced industrial countries will become increasingly reliant on for-profit advertising/marketing firms and techniques. First among these is the inability to reach the faithful through traditional Church-owned media. Most of what passes for Church-oriented media in the United States Catholic world remains print-based. Despite some occasional upturns in some numerical indicators (the number of U.S. diocesan newspapers grew from 163 in 1981 to 185 in 1993, for example), the overall health and reach of Church-owned or affiliated publications are dismal. Between 1985 and

1993, for example, three of the five largest national Catholic newspapers saw huge circulation drops (the other two gained fewer than a thousand subscribers each); among six national magazines, three saw huge losses, two others saw major (but somewhat less catastrophic) losses, with the last one posting only modest gains (Lynch 1993, p. 26). The total circulation figures for all Catholic media are minuscule compared to the size of the Catholic community in the United States—roughly half of which does not attend Mass on a regular basis (and thus beyond the reach of almost any Church-oriented print media).

For their part, diocesan media remain plagued by serious problems (see Goldman 1993, p. B-3; Fitzgerald 1989, pp. 34–5). Nearly all diocesan papers in the United States lose money; the Archdiocese of Los Angeles may close its papers in favor of a shift into cable television and direct mail, according to its communications director. Other diocesan papers are increasing their reliance on advertising (Johnson 1990, p. 40). Mandated quotas forced on parishes by bishops have kept circulation figures from falling even further in recent years (Lynch 1993, p. 26).

Some of the problems attendant to Church media are readily apparent: confused or contradictory objectives, censorship, chronic underfunding, and the like (Goldman 1993, p. B-5). Church media to date seem largely out of touch, behind the standards of media acceptability established by entertainment-oriented and -driven products. This may change as Church leaders feel pressed to enter the world of television and multimedia in a big way.

With its own media inadequate and minuscule, with information on religion and the Church coming via the channels of the culture industries, with most of their members far more involved as television viewers than Church members, Church leaders will almost surely increase their partnerships with (and reliance on) for-profit ad agencies, market research firms, and commercial media. Given the accommodative approach preferred by Church leaders, few other options seem available. Already the major culture industry players have taken positions in several existing religious cable television networks and content providers: Industry powerhouse TCI backed the ecumenical Faith and Values Channel in 1988 and helped Pat Robertson and his son start International Family Entertainment in 1990 (the Robertsons invested $180,000, while TCI's John Malone went in for $45 million). These and similar efforts are not direct moneymakers—no cable system operator will pay for a religious channel, given their small ratings (Kennedy 1995, pp. 97, 102). What for-profit cable firms do derive from these partnerships are good public relations, control over market share and product, and a superficial diversity in the programming package offered to local cable systems. In all, the weak, nearly desperate, position of the churches is apparent in these efforts to date.

It is not yet clear how far the Church will take its embrace of advertising, marketing, and other aspects of commercial culture industries. Will the Church sponsor in-depth psychological studies of the faithful in an attempt to see what symbols, songs, or stories might be "triggers" to increased contributions or Mass attendance? Will it follow the lead of professional sports teams that rename arenas to attract corporate sponsors, à la the United Center, Delta Center, and Fleet Center? (Can we expect the Waste Management/St. Paul's Parish, the Blockbuster/St. Peter's Basilica, or similar developments?) Such crudities seem beyond the pale, but the promotional options between here and there seem open for discussion. And those discussions are likely to be pushed ahead by the communication inadequacies of the Church and by structural weaknesses in Church finances.

The Corporate Christ?

As long as the Church has found large-scale property ownership and accumulation to be in its interest, conflicts between resource managers and religious enthusiasts have been part of the scene. The relative influence of conservative money managers relative to advocates of more radical gospel lifestyles and priorities has varied across time and place. In our time and place, as the Church seems to move closer to the practices of corporate culture industries, the scales will tip yet again in the direction of still greater power for the financial officers, accountants, and clerks—a resurgent variant of what Samuel Escobar calls "managerial missiology," a notion he describes as "an unduly pragmatic orientation which conceives of Christian mission as a manageable enterprise" (see Engel 1992, p. 21).

Much has been written about the various indices and contributors to the fiscal crisis in many branches of the Catholic Church—severe shortages of clerical labor, uneven or inadequate levels of lay participation, low per-capita levels of lay financial support, and more (see for example Greeley and McManus 1987). Several of the other trends and practices discussed in this chapter seem likely to empower further financial officers relative to other roles in the Church. The increased attractiveness of professional advertising, television, and other culture industry ventures will surely lead to greater demands for revenue, which in turn will likely lead to greater reliance on advertising, market research, and media to generate funds, and so on—the cycle, in other words of tele-evangelism. Raising money via the media in order to keep using media to raise money may no longer be limited, in the Catholic world, to the fiefdom of Mother Angelica's Eternal Word Television Network.

In Europe, those Churches that derive financial support from tax revenues (Germany and Italy among others) delimit and mute their social and political witness so as not to imperil their funding. In the United States, similar conservatising influences come from the desire to preserve tax-exempt status, government grants and contracts, and contributions from wealthy individuals and corporations. Within the Church, corporate/financial professional training is encouraged and rewarded at all levels; indeed, the president of the University of Notre Dame argues that one of the most important services that Catholic colleges and universities can provide to other Church institutions (parishes and dioceses, social service groups, lay movements, and the like) is to provide fundraising, management, and administrative training (Malloy 1990, pp. 104–5). Catholic institutions of higher learning are far more likely to churn out accountants than advocates, people more attuned to economics than evangelism.

With reference to diocesan and parish administration, business schools and Church consultants now point to the economic reengineering of the Archdiocese of Chicago as an example of "a restructuring and cost-containment campaign that would be the envy of any corporate chief" (Wangensteen 1996, p. 1). The plan eliminated one-tenth of the Archdiocesan schools, hiked tuition for those that remained, raised parish financial assessments due to the central office, and implemented a "new marketing plan" in some parishes, with the intent to attract young and affluent new members to old, hitherto-poor parishes. This latter move was to be driven by redirecting pastoral programming to fit the needs (professional and pastoral) of corporate executives and young professionals (Kelly 1991, pp. 61–2).

The architects of the plan were among the elite of Chicago's corporate community, including Eileen Corcoran (senior manager at Ernst and Young); Barry Sullivan (Chairman, First Chicago Corporation); Robert Galvin (Chairman, Motorola); R. Michael Murray (Director, McKinsey and Co.), and James Denny (Chief Financial Officer, Sears and Roebuck). According to one account, the late Joseph Cardinal Bernadin was so impressed with the group's plan that he ordered that "each parish would have a local [financial] council of parish business leaders" (Kelly 1991, p. 61).

Within the next few years, a full one-third of Chicago parishes had their own business managers (Wangensteen 1996, p. 34).

Nationally, 85 percent of Catholic high schools have full-time development directors, and corporate analogies and models are prevalent in the discourses of Catholic educators and administrators (Gonzalez 1993, p. A-1), as well as in diocesan and pastoral offices (Stewart 1989, p. 116). In turn, U.S. corporations have found that hiring full-time chaplains is a cost-effective boost to morale and profitability as firms pursue layoffs, downsizing, and "reengineering" (Heckler-Feltz 1993, p. 5). In this climate of increased corporate influence in Church affairs, capital-intensive moves into media, marketing, and the like seem certain to increase the power of financial experts to define the ecclesial agenda—what is "impractical," "imprudent," "too controversial," or "unpopular."

Toward a Catholic "Church Growth" Machine?

The aforementioned, considered together, have implications that promise to eviscerate further the fullness of the gospel. What is taking shape in broad outline—thus far more at the level of theory and/or disconnected practices than as coherent, integrated strategy—is a Catholic variant of the much-discussed "Church Growth" philosophy associated initially with evangelical churches in North America (but now a worldwide phenomenon). Given the negative connotations that Church Growth carries in most mainline Protestant and Catholic circles, the Catholic equivalent will doubtless have another name, or none at all. But it is not unrealistic, given the assumptions of Church leaders and the problems as they see them, that their solutions will look ominously like Church Growth in more respectable garb. I hope I am wrong, but the signs (at least in the Anglo precincts of the U.S. Catholic Church) are not altogether encouraging.

The Church Growth movement has been extensively analyzed elsewhere. For our purposes, it will suffice to describe it as an integrated strategy to increase church membership and income by utilizing the full array of marketing tools and research. Church activities, architecture, liturgy, and theology are then adapted to fit the preferences and desires of the target populations. As summarized by Gayle White:

> They study your lifestyle and appeal to your needs, drawing you into their churches with health clubs, support groups, singles dinners, or nursery schools for your children.

Recognizing that you like peppy music and positive sermons, they gear their worship to your taste.

In secular terminology, you're a consumer and God is their product. (White 1991, p. A-1)

Churches pursuing such strategies study and imitate the marketing, administration, and promotional strategies of firms like Disney, IBM, and Xerox (Niebuhr 1991, p. 1). The results, as exemplified by the Willow Creek Community Church, are so impressive in numerical and monetary terms as to resemble a fast-growing franchise operation new to the religious scene. That most of that growth (upward of 80 percent, according to Sidey 1991, p. 47) comes from defections from existing churches rather than attraction of previously unchurched persons, does not trouble most Church Growth advocates. It's simply an example of market share growth attendant to production and marketing of a superior experience of Christ.

James Engel is a marketing professor whose views on the uses of marketing by churches (such as in the Church Growth movement) have moved from broadly supportive to critical. Engel admits to being troubled by the theological acculturation that follows from churches that put audience/consumer sovereignty at the center of their efforts. As he notes, part of the lure of Church Growth-style approaches

lies in the area of appeal to felt need. People *do respond* when their felt needs are addressed in a way that does not call for an altogether different motivation and lifestyle. (Engel 1992, p. 23)

While such an approach is now supported by greater sophistication and powerful tools, it is not unknown in church history. Just in this century, the distance from Andrew Carnegie's "Gospel of Wealth" to Robert Schuller's *The Be-Happy Attitudes* is a short one. Engel adds:

It is possible to build a large church quickly and easily by promising that Jesus is the answer to your felt needs, your hopes and dreams. Crowds thronged around Jesus in his early ministry days because of this very expectation. As he focused on the narrow way, however—the meaning of kingdom living—those crowds dwindled. (Engel 1992, p. 23)

On one level, it is hard to imagine a multiethnic, multiclass phenomenon like the Catholic Church yielding to a variant of Church Growth on any appreciable level. But given the many problems outlined thus far, the increased attractiveness of marketing ideology and tools, and intensified competition from pentecostal and other movements (see Poewe 1994, for a transnational study), a high level of confidence seems even more unwarranted.

As hard as it may be to imagine a Catholic parish transformed by Church Growth thinking (the yuppie transformation of Old St. Patrick's in Chicago—in part produced by the Archdiocese's reengineering strategy—shows some similarities), so must it have been hard to anticipate the recent transformation of Denver's Full Gospel Chapel. Described as a "conservative bastion" by two evangelical observers, it reconstituted itself with a new mission and new name—"The Happy Church." According to the pastor, the new name "draws in people" in large numbers. So successful is the Happy Church that it recently took over a $7.8 million shopping mall in the Denver area (Colson and Vaughn 1992, p. 31). Perhaps the prospects for a Catholic Church Growth movement—Our Lady of the Mutual Fund, maybe?—are not so remote after all.

Religious Formation Amidst the Global Culture Industries

My belief that mainstream Christianity (Catholic and Protestant) needs a stronger ecclesiology is not dependent on (although it is reinforced by) my assessment of postfordist cultural ecology—I would argue for it independently of such considerations. But for those who believe the church must tack with the prevailing winds of cultural change on an ongoing basis, I want to give them a way over to my point of view. Even if one rejects my view that Christianity ought to hold a radical discipleship ethic as intrinsic to its practice, one might still see that—in an age of culture-industry overload, inundation, and cooptation—nothing but a stronger, more intensive, and formative practice of church is likely to sustain a Christianity worth continuing. In other words, if one aspires to a vision of life more similar to Jesus of Nazareth than Jim and Tammy Faye Bakker, one must inhabit a church distinct enough and strong enough to mitigate the effects of global culture industries.

With reference to the concerns of this book, one requisite in countering the effects of global culture industries is offering a church-centered prescription for religious formation conducted here within the belly of the postfordist cultural beast. Constructing a church-centered strategy for lifelong formation and learning is difficult on many levels; not surprisingly, then, many in the Church put forward more piecemeal, less controversial recommendations. Because these more modest proposals are most likely to dominate pastoral discussions, these should be examined before turning one's attention to the more fundamental rethinking of church life and practice I advocate and see as necessary in our time and place.

What Not to Do

More of the Same in Religious Education.   It is no insult to the volunteers and staff currently responsible for Christian education and formation to acknowledge the inadequacy of present arrangements. Persons of good will and dedication who work through CCD programs, most parish-based adult education programs, and what remains of the Catholic school system in countries like the United States are being asked to do the impossible. In a world in which for-profit culture industries monopolize the time and attention of nearly everyone, they must attempt to inculcate the gospel by way of underfunded, fragmented, and generally ineffectual means.

Longer appraisals of contemporary religious education/formation issues are available (see for example O'Malley 1990a; Sarno 1987). For now, I offer several reasons for believing that the status quo with regard to education/formation practices is both inadequate and inimical to generating more committed Christians.

Marcel Dumestre, Assistant Director of the Institute for Ministry at Loyola University in New Orleans, identifies several shortcomings in existing arrangements:

> We are a church at risk, and a primary reason is that adult Catholics are not literate about their religion. As a whole, Catholic adults do not know their religious heritage. Adult Catholics tend to operate with information about their religion that was gained in their childhood and teen-age years. Typically, Catholic adults have expanded their knowledge base in other areas of their lives, except for their religion. (Dumestre 1993, p.24)

One can overemphasize "religious literacy" or posit rationalist book-learning (like the new Catechism) as a solution; even Dumestre admits that a lack of "knowledge about" the faith is not a new Catholic problem

(1993, p. 24). My own emphasis would be less on religious *literacy* and more on religious *fluency*: not simply knowledge about but knowing how to think, feel, and pray through and with the symbols, stories, and characters of the tradition. Both learning *about* (the literacy problem) and learning *how* (the competence/fluency problem) are made worse by practices that taper off formation/education experiences as one approaches adulthood. Most adult speakers of a foreign language would be unsatisfied or underequipped to comprehend life with the linguistic repertoire of a child; yet we expect countless adult Christians to do something comparable. No wonder the results are what they are.

One consequence of focusing on children at the expense of adults is to render many adults—especially parents—incapable of being effective teachers, mentors, or evangelizers of their own children. Having themselves been shaped more by the global culture industries than by the Christian traditions, how can parents transmit anything other than a deeply compromised version of the faith without themselves being challenged, extended, and enriched by intensive, adult-centered confrontation with the gospel?

While some observers see signs of progress in this area (Orsi 1994, p. 398; Gibeau 1994), I remain convinced that religious education/formation remains a low priority within mainstream Catholicism in countries like the United States. Diocesan and parish budget cuts hit religious education staff early and often, and volunteer staff frequently lack adequate training or education for their jobs (Mongovern 1992, pp. 234, 238–9). The main vehicle for reaching children in secular schools, the Confraternity of Christian Doctrine (CCD) program, remains plagued by inadequate support and resources, high rates of nonparticipation or token participation, and uneven levels of staff competence and morale; at one extreme, one veteran CCD teacher agrees with her students that the program is "a waste of time," and should be redesignated as the "Central City Dump" (CCD) program (Denman 1992, p. 210; her account of life as a CCD teacher may be more typical than her strong rhetoric suggests).

Matters with adults fare little better, insofar as the typical adult religious program "tends to be the least systematic and most underfunded parish or school program," to such an extent that "even the term adult religious education is [now] a turnoff for many people" (Dumestre 1993, p. 27).

For both children and adults, practices of religious education/formation are sabotaged by confused, contradictory, and consistently low expectations. With reference to Catholic schools, Marian Crawford and Graham Rossiter observe that

> regardless of how important it is in the school's mission statement, religious education is not always regarded by many parents or students as a necessary or valuable pursuit—certainly not one that could make a difference when getting a job; neither is it always seen as making a major contribution to quality of life. Interestingly, most of the same students will say that religion as such is important—the sort of nominal religion that is better to have than not to have, just in case! (Crawford and Rossiter 1995, pp. 70–1)

The low expectations manifested in existing religious education/formation efforts fit comfortably with the minimalist ecclesiology I find so inadequate. In such a subordination of the gospel to the values and goals of the market, the state, and other regnant social forces, all that one requires of education/formation is that such produce church members who are "good" people as defined by these other powers. Such is almost constitutive of a civil religion that blesses and nourishes existing social and political arrangements, but it is far indeed from the life and practice of Jesus. Existing practices of religious education/formation may be adequate to produce believers of this sort; to move beyond that is to invite opposition from parents, many episcopal leaders, and secular powerholders who are attentive to shifts in the ecclesial winds.

"Just Turn It Off".   A second dead-end solution to the problems of symbolic overload and spiritual incoherence is to posit individual withdrawal as the solution. This is the churchly equivalent to the culture industries' response to any and all criticism: "If you don't like it, turn it off."

Would that it were so easy. If only the Pope's halfhearted call for occasional TV abstinence during Lent (1996, p. 1) could really be an opening for the church to relearn and create anew its own stories and songs, images, and habits. As it is, however, such appeals look like little more than handwaving at a problem only half-understood. As if the mediated flood stopped with an individual turning off a TV (while everyone else in his/her world continues in the swim). As if such appeals, divorced from serious and intensive discussion among the faithful about the specifically Christian reasons for such withdrawal, were likely to help congregations see the issues affecting the vitality of the church as a community rather than a concern for some persons "as individuals" (e.g., children, heavy consumers, the "unsophisticated"). And as if abstinence (whether temporary or permanent) by itself could help us absorb more fully and deeply the affections and dispositions of Jesus, absent radical changes in the church itself.

By themselves, abstinence/"turn-off" tactics contribute to the misperception of media effects as primarily problems of and for individuals. Such advice ignores the degree to which becoming a Christian remains a lifelong project that for most of us requires other Christians as partners in instruction, dialogue, mutual correction, and encouragement. One cannot internalize the language of Christian life when all other believers are submerged in the culture industries' tide of jingles, plots, and logos. And even if done more or less completely (no TV or radio, magazines, or Internet) and more or less indefinitely, such is no guarantee that the thus-liberated time and attention will be devoted to processes of Christian formation; that would require far more of the church than is assumed under a "turn it off" strategy.

"If You Can't Beat 'Em . . . ". This third no-win suggestion suggests that the way to counter the effects of global culture industries on the church is for the church to use such means for its own purposes. Much of this chapter's critique of sacramental liberalism and the evangelization fixation applies here as well, albeit with an ecumenical twist: both Protestantism (old-line and evangelical) and Catholicism embrace this strategy in its many variants.

What becomes apparent in reviewing many of the voices calling for active, enhanced church involvement in culture industries as presently constituted is the utter modesty of their ultimate goals. The more sober among them recognize that commercial media cannot make Christians, cannot help form disciples in any important fashion, and cannot proclaim the radical nature of the gospels. What they can do is often described as "pre-evangelization," described by one major analyst as giving "information about the Christian faith" and ensuring that "the right questions" are raised in society. At best, culture industries can act as "preparation for the gospel," which involves three stages: presenting media explorations of those "boundary situations" of life where modern people experience a lack of "meaning"; affirming in the media "persons and events that have been able to deal with these 'boundary situations' creatively and with faith"; and third, "it requires pointing to the churches as the place where people can go to begin to work out their salvation, find community, and discover the power of confession and forgiveness" (Fore 1990, pp. 81–2).

Such a limited set of expectations, which sees television (for example) as "a signpost, a servant of the local church—and never the other way around" (Fore 1990, p. 82), is increasingly overshadowed by broader, more society-centered goals. The churches should utilize commercial culture industries to reclaim their role as the moral center, helping society with questions of shared "values" and "meaning." This call to help postfordist societies deal with their problems of meaning and common purpose—yet another form of chaplaincy, of the church defining its mission as being useful to existing social arrangements and institutions—echoes throughout mainstream literature on church and media.

For example, in the experience of Canada's VISION TV network, "the world's first national multifaith and multicultural network," the objective is to examine life from the perspective of "ethics" and "values." And if the question of whose ethics or whose values—let alone the particularity and practices of the church—becomes awkward in the search for one-size-fits-all public language, VISION TV's president proudly reports that the majority of the network's programs "are not perceived to be 'religious' at all," rather, cultural, educational, or spiritual. They attract a broad general audience (Keast 1990, p. 34). What particularity there is on the network comes from paying customers of the religious (Anglicans, Buddhists, Muslims, Jains, Catholics, Mennonites, Sikhs, and more) and commercial variety (advertisers); the latter "want to reach the older, well-educated and well-off audiences" the network delivers (Keast 1990, p. 35).

Lest one assume that the concern with "values" programming becomes too tiresome, Keast assures us that

> VISION TV provides Canadians with lots of entertaining programming. We do not concentrate on the "worry of the week." Being alternative does not mean having no audience. We are not meeting any of our objectives if we are talking to ourselves. Nor will we stay in business very long. Even though we are a distinctly different and alternative service, like all television we must understand and appeal to our audiences. (Keast 1990, p. 36)

Maybe not so "distinctly different and alternative" after all?

VISION TV in Canada is the inspiration for the Faith and Values Network (VISN) (recently renamed the Odyssey network) in the United States, a major interfaith cable network featuring a similar blend of civil religion and sponsored specificity. That such networks do present interesting and occasionally "challenging" programs is not the point; by reinforcing the liberal myth that media tools exist in a decontextualized, power-free world, advocates for such approaches minimize the corrosive effects of those same culture industries on the "faith and values" traditions they hope to make relevant to a media-saturated world. Such instrumentalism leads to some pathetic ironies, as when the final report of an interfaith/media professional conference on "Religion, Television, and the Information Superhighway" had the "Religion Group" arguing for a bigger piece of the media pie for their constituencies, leaving it to the media professionals in the "Television Group" to worry about "the impact of the media on the formation of both individual and societal values, whether ethical or spiritual," and about the adverse effects on religious communities from the pervasiveness of culture industries (Shayon and Cox 1994, pp. 6–7).

However legitimate—in theory—may be the large-scale adoption of culture industries' tools as "servants of the local church," in practice too often the dynamic seems to be inverted. Instead of leading people to the church—and there is no evidence I know of that reports positive correlations between old-line religious programming and revitalized local congregations, for example—strategies that hope to restore the vitality of the churches using the tools of the culture industries seem doomed to failure or frustration. These tools do not exist independent of their institutional settings, and audiences do not encounter church media productions unformed by commercial ones; together, these considerations make it more likely that churches that adopt the tools of the dominant culture industries do nothing to help make the gospel a lived, viable option in the world. Churches opting for the "If you can't beat 'em, join 'em" choice guarantee their own cultural irrelevance, consigning themselves to the role of ineffectual nannies urging—in a weak, timid voice—that powerful actors be "kinder and gentler" with those they exploit.

Search for a Silver Bullet: Media Literacy/Education

Programs in media literacy and/or media education are important in any consideration of reclaiming competence and voice in media-saturated cultures. Across the political and theological spectrum, one or another version of media literacy is proffered as a necessary response to a long list of problems connected in one way or another to media products, processes, or institutions. As part of a larger, comprehensive vision, many media literacy programs are valuable and legitimate undertakings. Regrettably, however, media literacy is being asked to carry too heavy a load, to be the "silver bullet" that by itself can slay the multiple demons drawn from the netherworld of the culture industries.

Media education or media literacy can be described as "a multitude of context and content-specific pedagogies," which are directed toward

- a critical understanding of global and local media realities including their structures, processes, and value-orientations;
- the creation of participatory, empowering discourses aimed at a broad cross-section of society;
- the formation of an active, discriminating public, linked to a citizens' movement for democratic media reform;
- the establishment of "alternative" media voices at a variety of levels. (*Media Development* 1995, p. 2)

Media literacy programs typically aim to teach "about" media rather than simply "with" them. Most attempt to encourage people to reflect on whether and how media affect attitudes and values, how they impact public life, and how persons and groups might discern and resist persuasion and propaganda campaigns from a variety of sources.

With regard to television, for example, media literacy aims (among other things) to encourage "critical viewing."

> Put simply it means helping children [for example] understand what goes into the making of a television program: how cameras are used to create mood, how action is used to advance a story, how suspense is created and so on. (Zukowski 1993a, p. 262)

While some media literacy programs and curricula limit their attention to media content and production techniques, the more comprehensive ones situate such within sustained study of structural relations (e.g., corporate oligopolies, deregulation, commercial imperatives; see Masterman 1995, p. 6). These programs and resources—which attempt to illustrate the linkages between macro- and micro-level phenomena with regard to culture industries—are important as part of how the Christian churches can equip themselves with the means to understand and counteract the cultural forces inhibiting the formation of more radical Christian communities and practices.

What are not helpful, however, are approaches to media literacy

- that envision it as the once-and-for-all solution to life in the commercial cultural flow;

- that seek to institutionalize it within school curricula (secular or parochial) rather than centered in the church proper;
- that ignore the extent to which many programs in media literacy presuppose goals that are irrelevant, secondary, or even damaging to those the church should seek in promoting media literacy.

Although no one in the media literacy/education movement would plead guilty to the first of these, many appear unduly optimistic as to the benefits flowing from media awareness programs. The latter two concerns, however, speak more directly to the limits of media literacy as a means by which the church can be more engaged in forming people shaped by the stories of the gospel.

For example, I would suggest that mass public education—oriented as it is in advanced industrial countries toward social control, service to the labor market, and socialization in national and capitalist myth (see Holt 1981; Apple 1990; Giroux and McLaren 1989)—cannot teach media literacy in ways adequate to the purposes of the church. Yet the primary focus of much, if not most, media education advocacy is on schools. Church leaders advocate for school-based efforts (e.g., the Australian Catholic Bishops in 1979; see Pungente 1996), and major efforts like the Jesuit Communications Project are focused on developing school-based programs throughout Canada and providing text and teacher materials for those programs (Pungente 1994, 1996).

I do not argue that no benefits will flow from school-based (as opposed to church-based) efforts at media literacy. I do argue that if incorporated into school curricula as yet another discipline in which "facts" and "values" are treated as separable components, media literacy will fall far short of its own ambitions and will be irrelevant to the purposes of church renewal in the mediated age.

More obviously in media literacy than in other school-based curricula, one cannot separate "facts" and "values," liberal wishes notwithstanding. And where media literacy is not joined to explicitly Christian goals, it invariably substitutes other, oftentimes competing, ones (like strengthening capitalist democracy, enhancing citizenship, creating more sophisticated consumers). These latter goals are abundantly featured even in materials urging greater church support for media literacy efforts.

For example, a document addressed to the "European Churches" by an important Euro-level working group of Christian communicators listed among its major objectives helping the public "to make freer choices, more responsible choices" regarding television program selection. Additionally, the group argued that formation efforts should help turn people into "responsible citizens" better able to engage in and support democratic public affairs (Audiovisual Media Education 1995, pp. 29–30). This group calls for a consumer-rights approach to media, with Associations of Television Viewers to be organized, funded, and aimed at advancing the notion of media in the public service (Audiovisual Media Education 1995, p. 29). The role of the churches in such efforts should be to support such consumer-rights efforts, serve families and individuals in becoming active consumers, and promote such citizenship-enhancing efforts of media literacy (pp. 31–2).

A better fitting late-Constantinian job description one cannot imagine for the churches in the media age: be useful to the political order and its deified self-description ("democracy"); prove one's value as a "service" to autonomous individuals and families, whose priorities and preferences continue to be formed independently of the church and gospel; and acquiesce in the atrophy of Christian language and formation in favor of more "universal" and "public" ones drawn from market and nationalist ideology.

What is true of media education efforts is also true, in varying degrees, of all the dead-end answers outlined in this chapter. Some of them have some contributions to make, some of them can be useful for Christian groups negotiating their way through postmodern cultures. But none of these approaches, as usually articulated, see the need for prior changes *within the churches*—for radical renewal, for a more intensive ecclesiology, for a reclaimed awareness of the differences being Church should entail— so that their tools might help. A church-centered approach to formation and postfordist culture can help salvage some of the worthwhile elements of the approaches outlined in this chapter, while radically reconfiguring them in a context of discipleship and Christian practice. We should examine what such an approach ought to include, in at least outline form, in the final chapter of this book.

7

The Way from Here:
Radical Gospel, Radical Church

Restoring a passionate, world- and person-transforming experience of faith to the center of Catholic and Christian practice defies easy solution. There exists no menu of options, no prefabricated dictates sure to reverse the effects of global culture industries and accommodationist theology. While I will sketch a few broad considerations that I believe will be important in moving ahead, collective efforts at crafting more adequate ecclesial responses are themselves part of being and building a different kind of church. Various ways of constructing more radical Christian communities in postfordist cultures will only emerge from the dialogues, interactions, and mutual challenges that flow within and between churches that emphasize their distinctiveness and subversive character, or they will not emerge at all.

The implication of Chapter 6 is that neither media-centered tactics nor religious education as conventionally practiced is up to the challenges facing the church in postfordist cultures. Unless Catholics and other Christians make their lives as a called, gathered community of disciples, a people "on the way," their *primary* point of reference and identity, the gospel will remain emaciated and marginalized by the effects of culture industries, militarized patriotism, capitalism, and other systems of exclusion and domination. Absent a church-centered renewal movement, the next generation will find progressively fewer Christian communities worth inhabiting and fewer still capable of sending forth persons committed to the poor, the exploited, or the powerless in the ways Jesus exemplified.

Part of the path from the Constantinian church type, which still dominates in advanced industrial regions, to a church of disciples involves a new discourse that puts the church at the center of Christian self-description. We must help bring into being a church in which Christian membership and identity is privileged over competing claims—as citizens of states/empires, as bar-coded consumers, or as political/sociological/ideological partisans. This involves seeing the church as a called and distinct community, an alternative, countercultural, or minority polis.

The new discourse invites Christians to be an ongoing experiment in how to work, play, disagree, love, and cooperate without the underlying recourse to violence and exploitation that lie within the systems of states and markets. The church as polis neither expects perfection nor punishes failure (failure is both expected and inevitable) in its alternative way of life, but unlike accommodationist tactics such as "dual ethic" and "evangelical counsels" thinking, which lower the demands of the gospel to a least-common (and inoffensive) denominator, the newer vision of church joins high hopes with mutual assistance, encouragement, and acceptance/forgiveness. Such a stance is imperative for a church that seeks to employ and not discard Jesus' practices/teachings on nonviolence, leadership as service and sacrifice, economic mutuality, and radical inclusiveness. The church is called to embody new possibilities, options not available to systems of power that presuppose the power to kill or torture in the name of "order," "freedom," "justice," or similar icons of idolatry, for it is against such institutionalized idolatry, which lays claims of ultimate allegiance on human bodies and affections, that the church must stand, now and until the culmination of the true Kingdom of God.

A vision and experience of church as the primary source for Christian self-definition and mission in the world presumes that the Church can and should change, even as it holds fast to the stories, poetry, and symbols of Jesus and the Christian tradition—a paradoxical charge to some, a contradictory one to others (although see Brueggemann 1982, for how the interplay between preservation and innovation shaped the Hebrew Scriptures and the history of Israel). For many people, urging that we embrace a tighter ecclesiology, especially in times of papal authoritarianism and centralization, sounds like a summons to move more deeply into a conservative, hierarchical, and patriarchal church model that stifles the Spirit, marginalizes women, and buttresses clerical power. While I understand the origins of the associations, given the appropriation of church-centered discourse by the "conservative" (but thoroughly modernist) wing of the Church, I maintain that a discipleship-focused Church can and should presuppose authority but not authoritarianism and that prioritizing the Church as one's primary formative group does not require accepting existing patterns of papal and hierarchical power, sexism, or other contingent aspects of the ecclesial status quo. Indeed, to the extent that the Church universal—Catholic, Orthodox, and Protestant—moves toward making formation and discipleship normative for all baptized Christians (not merely for the few), one can expect substantial anxiety or determined opposition from the more authoritarian sectors of the Church as presently constituted. In a discipleship polis, people will need one another's talents and efforts *more*, not less, than under present arrangements; the Christian community will not have the luxury to exclude, ignore, or marginalize fellow believers on the bases of gender, race, class, or other arbitrary stratifications.

The topics of authority and authoritarianism require further discussion. When I argue that the churches need a stronger ecclesiology, a self-definition that calls people to a more devoted and wide-ranging practice of discipleship, I am *not* calling for a single (nor a fundamentalist) reading of scripture, unchanging notions of orthodoxy, or blind obedience to formal authority. This important distinction, analyzed by Robin Perrin and Armand Mauss (1993), derives from the insights of Dean Kelley's hugely important *Why Conservative Churches are Growing* (1972). Kelley insisted on distinguishing between the social *strength* of churches ("reflected in member commitment, discipline, and evangelical zeal") and their *strictness* ("reflected in absolutism, conformity, and fanaticism") (Perrin and Mauss 1993, p. 125). Kelley maintained that the two were distinct in theory and practice, a position supported by Perrin and Mauss's recent empirical work. Their conclusion—that a church strong in commitment, energy, and disciplined practices need not be intolerant, punitive, or mindless— accords with the position I have argued for several years.

To say that Christianity is like a language that one internalizes, through which one gains the means to experience, appreciate, and express things often unavailable to those lacking such competence, is not to insist that only one way of speaking that language, or only one usage pattern, is acceptable. Any language is enriched by a variety of accents, and all languages sustain their vitality through the interplay of local idioms and expressions, yet still the language remains recognizably the same to its competent users. It remains capable of spinning webs of shared meaning, the capacity for comprehensible disputes, and a context for virtuosity and innovation.

For the Christian scriptures and stories to serve as a primary formative language, a similar degree of flexibility, bounded variety, and novelty is both assured and required. Brueggemann invites Christian communities to develop their own midrashic styles of biblical interpretation as a way to give greater importance to scripture-as-formative without enforcing a single, coerced interpretation (1995, pp. 314–6). Multiple readings or interpretations of scripture, to him and others, are normal and should not be seen as a "problem"; not reading or attending to these potent texts is by far a more serious "problem" for the contemporary church.

Similarly, Nadine Pence Frantz points to the power of community testimonials of faith as a powerful, noncoercive way of forming more committed Christian communities in postmodern cultures. As she describes it, the testimonial is

> a narrative of a people whose self-perception was primarily defined by its interaction with God . . . The intent of the whole [Bible] is testimonial, including a rhetorical function designed to evoke a response of appropriation. In other words, Scripture is seen as that which was told and recorded with the intent to evoke a similar life and faith in other people. It is intended to evoke an encounter. (Frantz 1994, p. 158)

Such a form of storytelling

> does not link revelation with the necessity of discovering a single meaning that was intended by the author of the [biblical] text, nor to the recovery of the received meaning of the text by the original author. Yet the category of testimonial does not set aside the use of critical methods . . . But although historical criticism is an important tool, it is not the location of revelation . . . the focus of revelation must be on the trust of the rhetorical function of the text in shaping and directing the present rhetorical community. (Frantz 1994, p. 158)

Seeing narratives of discipleship and witness as invitations to emulation accords with Michael Warren's proposals for creating a church strong enough to resist the corrosive effects of for-profit culture industries. As he notes,

> Gospel proposals cannot be imposed from without; they must be embraced from within, and for most of us, even then, one step at a time, tentatively, feeling our way. Close-knit communities may not agree on specific lines of response and action. The best way of proposing a line of action to anyone is

not via the "shoulds" and "musts" of imperatives but via provocative descriptions of a particular situation, of the various ways it may be interpreted, and of our options in responding to it. There are many such examples in the open-ended sort of proposals and invitations we find in the Gospels. (Warren 1995, pp. 26–7)

I do not wish to avoid the inevitable tension between the desire for a stronger sense of church and respect for church diversity. And I am aware of the irony of our age, in which a loose official ecclesiology combines with arbitrary exercises of hierarchical authority to make people distrustful of *any* calls for a stronger notion of church (in Kelley's sense). If the present is how authority operates (in a *weak*-ecclesiology church, no less), imagine how much worse life would be in a discipleship-based church—purges, prosecutions, "shunnings," and the like! I do not accept the linkages made in such reasoning, but I am not blind to why many people would make them.

Given this, it is crucial that the development of more intensive Christian communities not be a project pursued primarily (and certainly not exclusively) by institutional leaders in the Church. Some Church leaders may be tempted to pursue such efforts only in a token fashion, or (at the other extreme) they will be pursued with a vengeance as a way to protect a narrow theological (but politically and socially accommodated) picture of the faith that insulates existing relations from change. As Virginia Hoffman notes, many of the lay-based discipleship initiatives in the Church seek to live out their baptismal call "to be faithful to the covenant, to serve and support without domination, to be a sign of hope and good news in our world" (1992, p. 201). This is often far removed from episcopal priorities that include saving the parish form or preserving the existing structures of the church in a (celibate male) priest-short time.

Both lay and clerical groups have contributions to make to the creation of churches able to fashion Christians against the flood of global culture industries. The need, now and into the foreseeable future, is to make Christian formation—as a discourse and a set of practices—the center of church life. Without such changes in self-definition and behavior, we can expect to see even further diminution of Christianity as it shrinks and hollows out in reaction to the processes described in earlier chapters. The language of faith, unless brought more fully and intensively into people's hearts and minds, will become as dead as Latin in our world of jingles, spectacles, and nonstop sales pitches.

Resisting the Culture Industries:
A Workshop of Witnesses

When I say that the church must put formation of all Christians at the heart of its discourse and practice, I emphatically reject any mass production or factory implications that some might read into the terms. "Creating Christians" is *not* a mass-production undertaking, one size fits all, and no amount of ecclesial or liturgical engineering can substitute for the ungovernable spark of the Spirit that must, at some point, convert the Church's efforts from potentialities to actualities. More appropriate might be images of a workshop of craft production, one person at a time, with different groups of people requiring differing modes of training and teaching—with the further wrinkle that the craftspersons themselves are unfinished, are themselves "on the way" of Christian discipleship and practices. The Christian faith, as a *verbum externum*, requires initiation, instruction, and imitation as requisites for internalization and virtuoso improvisation; a one-size-fits-all approach to formation, such as efforts that run roughshod over the diverse experiences of ethnic, racial, and other diversities within the Church is just as unhelpful as the present ecclesial situation in which formation is mostly trivialized, superficial, or routinized.

As noted by Ellen Charry:

> The church is perhaps the only institution with the beliefs, literature, liturgy, practices, social structure, and authority (diminished though it may be) necessary to rescue children [and adults?] from the violence and other deforming features of late 20th century life. But it cannot accomplish this simply by laying the faith before young people and inviting them to choose it. Nor can it impose Christian identity by force and indoctrination. It can only prepare the setting for the Holy Spirit slowly to nurture children into Christian faith and practice. Churches need to think creatively about how to assist the Spirit in this process of formation. (Charry 1994, p. 166)

I am not an expert in pastoral practice, but I feel it important to offer a few suggestions that might be part of efforts to advance discipleship in postmodern cultures. Only responses that begin with changes in church identity and practice stand capable of addressing the various sorts of corrosion traceable (in various measure) to the global culture industries. The following suggestions should start, not end, the discussion.

The Church as Vision/Perception Clinic

One need not be a scripture scholar to notice how many stories and refer-
ences in the New Testament concern "blindness," learning to "see" the
world in new ways, and becoming able to "recognize" God's way in the
world (the Hebrew Scriptures, while also attentive to vision, place special
emphasis on being able to "hear" God and God's word). In our day, in
which corporations and governments spend billions of dollars annually to
colonize our senses and dazzle our perceptions, the church must become
something of a "vision" or "perceptions" clinic capable of removing cultural blinders and letting the radical Jesus shine through in all His en-
trancing, dangerous glory. Viewing the church's mission in these terms requires us to admit that our existing pictures of Jesus and the faith have
been far too tame, constructed more to our own comfort and self-interest
than as a reflection of someone executed by the state, vilified by the economic and religious elites of his day, and identified with the rejects of society. Learning to see Jesus and his ministry anew at first involves making
the familiar seem strange, the obvious seem opaque, the uncontroversial
seem contentious. Learning to see, in other words, may well begin with
challenging what passes for sight and reality in the eyes of the world (inside and outside the church). The pictures of reality that are the daily
bread of the global culture industries, in the phrase of Melanie May, involve "an obliteration of the *imago Dei* in all but the privileged few pro-
tected by state and corporate institutions" (1994, p. 35). Learning to see as
Christians presupposes a training that enables us to see the image of God
in all God's people, especially those too insignificant to be noticed by the
reality-shapers of the world.

Calling for an ecclesiology that puts an alternative way of seeing at
the heart of church life can remain stuck at the level of generalization.
To give flesh to this notion, I offer a few more specific recommendations.

The Lifelong Catechumenate.   As discussed in Chapter 4, the catechumenate process in the pre-Constantinian church was a serious, demanding
period of personal transformation and initiation. It assumed that the
Christian way could be adopted only with the help of mature, experienced
mentors; conflict with other goals and groups (even one's own family) was
accepted and predictable as a matter of course. Michael Warren describes
the three-year catechumenate as

a period of therapy meant to ensure that each person did embody a Christian imagination that could be lived out in a particular way. This was a period of restructuring the "affect" of the candidate. Re-imagining ourselves involves re-learning our ways of evaluating reality and our emotional responses to it. The catechumenate, then, was a time for assuring a life of fidelity to Jesus' imagination of the world. (Warren 1988b, p. 382)

After centuries of neglect, the Catholic Church revitalized the catechetical experience for adult converts through the RCIA (Rite of Christian Initiation for Adults) program. This program reflects the need for "a whole new way of instilling Catholic identity in new members," insisting upon "a much longer and more gradual process for coming to membership" (Duggan 1994, pp. 111, 113). RCIA represents a view of Christian membership that makes formative processes central and explicit. As Robert Duggan observes:

> Not only has the time of formation been extended, but there is a much more deliberate attempt today to lead prospective members through a progressive process in which slowly escalating demands are made upon them. The message is clear: Catholic identity is something that one assumes gradually and is not merely a question of giving assent to our doctrinal synthesis. (Duggan 1994, p. 113)

What the Church prescribes for converts, I propose—in various and diverse formats—for all Catholics (and all Christians, for that matter). What the Church requires for a limited time prior to initiation, I propose as a lifelong (but not incessant) undertaking. As many Christian converts can attest, those baptized as infants in a tradition are often sorely in need of catechetical formation, so casual and insignificant is Christianity in their lives. And unless processes of formation extend beyond the converts and the young to include adult members and cradle Catholics—unless all in the church recognize their need for ongoing maturation and enrichment, teaching, and learning, and ever-growing risk-taking and fidelity— the church will continue to merely baptize the culture instead of challenging it with the gospel.

A lifelong catechumenate, as an explicit program of Christian formation, makes transparent the nearly invisible processes of consumerist formation and postmodern dissolution. As Michael Warren notes, formation must be seen "as a social and cultural fact of life" practiced by powerful corporate institutions and processes, as well as by religious communities (Warren 1987a, p. 515). The major difference between capitalist and Christian formation centers on whether claims of ultimate value are made overtly (as in religious traditions) or covertly (as in capitalism).

> The problem is that the covert claims can be more powerful because, never explicitly made, they are harder to identify and resist . . . [As a result] we tend not just to overlook what is happening, but to be unable to notice. (Warren 1987a, p. 523)

Since all Christians, converts or not, are inundated by the covert formation processes of the culture industries, all can benefit from the purifying and restructuring of affections, desires, and imagination associated with classical and contemporary catechesis.

I hope to encourage persons more skilled and experienced in formation/religious education to develop programs for lifelong catechesis. There is no reason to suppose that only one approach or model will suit all congregations and groups; indeed, local churches or dioceses might find great formative value in creating, adapting, or extending their own efforts at Christian nurture. With that in mind, I offer the following generalizations, which may be helpful to some in this regard.

Catechesis and Conversion.   Catechesis aimed at the baptized, contrary to some, does not intend to produce mindless serfs, slaves to authority. As William O'Malley notes, we in the church are about recruiting and training shepherds, not sheep. What separates shepherds—which we are all called to be—from sheep, in his view, is the experience of conversion, an internalization and profound appropriation of the gospel in ways that reorient one's whole life (1990a, pp. 2–4).

One can understand conversion in diverse ways, but Mary O'Keefe offers one helpful definition:

> Christian conversion is the total—if never entirely complete—surrender of the person to God as revealed in Jesus Christ. Christian conversion, as the continual process of self-surrender to God in Christ, therefore encompasses every aspect of the Christian life and necessarily grounds the moral and spiritual efforts of every Christian. (O'Keefe 1995, p. 4)

Further, she adds, "conversion to Christ is also conversion to the reign of God that Jesus came to announce" (1995, pp. 4–5).

Commitment to conversion as the primary goal of pastoral effort goes far beyond those whose goals are to keep young people going to church, to assure lockstep obedience to the Pope and bishops on all issues, or to maintain the fiscal viability of the parish form. Lifelong catechesis, I suggest, is part of what Vincent Donovan calls "the refounding of the Church of Jesus Christ for our age"—far beyond church reform or revival (1992, p. 216).

Conversion in the Catholic tradition may take many forms—charismatic and expressive, quiet and contemplative, dramatic or gradual. However it comes, it involves accepting the Christian story

> as the most credible interpretation of life's meaning and purpose . . . Gradually, the transformed vision of Christian conversion deepens the transformation of the Christian so that he or she develops distinctively Christian perspectives, dispositions, affections, intentions, priorities. (O'Keefe 1995, p. 9)

Far from a feel-good burst of religious enthusiasm that underwrites a life of spiritual self-justification, the conversion we should prize is destabilizing of worldly hierarchies of value and is tied to radical witness on behalf of those denigrated or ignored by the powerful.

> In short, Christian conversion, and the path of ongoing conversion on which it establishes a person, involves a conformity to the cross. Like Jesus, the disciple seeks continual self-giving in a world of limit and of sin. Embracing the cross involves the acceptance of suffering that cannot be avoided, the sometimes painful self-surrender entailed in loving service of others, the taking up of the discipline that a sustained life of prayer requires, the acceptance of the purgation that advanced prayer brings, and the self-sacrifice involved in courageous action on behalf of justice. (O'Keefe 1995, p. 10)

Radical Conversion, Time, and Attention.   Contrary to the cheap grace and instant gratification proffered by many television preachers, Christian conversion is not a fast-food commodity. Instant conversion fits well with the cultural ecology of the global culture industries—in which every experience or thrill is just a credit card's length away—but it will not form disciples able and willing to challenge the powers of our world. That sort of formation requires a deeper and more fundamental sort of conversion, which rarely emerges except as an unpredictable dividend of time and attention invested in disciplined practices.

Time and attention, of course, are the primary targets of the global culture industries. The amusements, enticements, and mentoring of advertising, television, and the like all require the "orchestration of attention," in Warren's phrase, in order to prosper. It is here that the conflict between Christian practice and the culture industries is most irreconcilable—each gains time and attention at the expense of the other. It is zero-sum, no compromise.

A discipleship-oriented church, the possibility of more fundamental conversion among already-baptized Catholics and other Christians, is simply impossible unless the church wins back time and attention from the global culture industries. Doing so requires both a reduction of hours spent involved with for-profit media (recall the depressing statistics from Chapter 5 on television hours, advertising, saturation, etc.) and an increase in involvement in church-based practices, learning, and apprenticeship.

Given the existing imbalances in time spent in "religious" activities compared to engagement with the culture industries in advanced industrial countries, the status quo is a one-way ticket to spiritual triviality or near-evaporation. As O'Malley ruefully observes, "Add up all the hours priests, nuns, and parents have spoken about religious values [to young people] and compare that to the countless hours TV, billboards, and movies have *demonstrated* material values, and the Church loses hands down" (1990a, p. 138).

The transfer of time and attention from the culture industries to lifelong catechesis cannot be mandated or coerced. Few church leaders perceive the incompatibility between the Gospel of Jesus and the Gospel of Pleasure in such oppositional terms. And even if they did, discipleship cannot be imposed, ordered, or mandated upon another person—it can only be modeled, illustrated in one's own life, joined with the invitation "Come and see" (Jn 1:39). A lifelong catechumenate represents a lifelong invitation to learn more, do more, risk more, and become more fully a herald of the Kingdom of God that Jesus proclaimed and discerned. The pastoral musicians and poets, storytellers and artists, social activists and prophets—those, in other words, who attempt to feed the Spirit's flame of gospel enthusiasm in themselves and others—must find ways for the elusive but undeniable attractiveness of Jesus to gain a hearing and draw attention in our novel cultural environment. Feeding that flame takes time and requires attentiveness—it cannot be accomplished during commercial breaks or while channel surfing.

Conversion and Smaller Ecclesial Structures.   No matter what one's church cause or concern, the answer these days seems to involve calls for "intentional communities," "base communities," "small groups," "church cells," "para-ecclesial formations," or some similar formulation. In pointing to the necessity for communal, more intensive interpersonal church interactions as a means to create a context for lifelong catechesis and conversion, I am aware that the existing popularity of small-group religion carries its own set of risks and dangers. Small groups are easily romanticized and idealized (Dumestre 1995, p. 204), they are proffered simplistically as solutions for a wide range of concerns, and they can foster a feel-good sort of Christianity that baptizes (rather than challenges) the economic and political self-interest of their mostly middle-class participants (in the United States) (on the general point see Wuthnow 1994, pp. 812–16; Dumestre 1995, pp. 198–9).

While not all small-group Christianity is countercultural, it appears that the goal of radical discipleship requires some experiences best evidenced in smaller, base-community-like settings. A lifelong catechumenate would seem to be most adequately conducted within and among such communities. The base-community model popularized by the Latin American church has been the most studied and heralded (and often oversold) example in recent years, but other sorts of small-group Christian practice may also be instructive when considering various ways to structure a lifelong catechetical process. A few such examples may be helpful.

Didier Piveteau, a French expert on religious education and formation, is convinced that current practices in Western Europe and the United States are doomed to failure. To him, "the most urgent task nowadays is to work at building a Church where initiation is possible. It means we have to find what *type of community* can be valid for the Church today" (1986, p. 26).

The larger society, which is "foreign to Christianity," cannot and should not be that sort of community. Neither is the family, nor the modern parish—the latter being a rural form that fails as a formative institution in urban areas. Instead,

> the future of Christian community therefore can only be a *free* gathering of people, composed of families, single parents, celibates, transcending neighborhood or work-teams and brought together only in the name of shared faith and hope (p. 28).

Such communities, to Piveteau, require four conditions to be alive and effective (pp. 28–9):

1. Small in size (no more than 50 or 80 people, in his formulation);

2. Not limited only to the spiritual dimension, "because then they are no longer real human communities, displaying values in everyday life and capable of being matrices of initiation." To be true communities, they must involve some sharing of time, goods/money, and culture;

3. Communities "should not aim at being long-lasting, encompassing the whole life of people. They serve a limited purpose for a time and then are replaced by something else."

4. They should not be centered or dependent upon an ordained priest for their maintenance and existence. Formative communities, he says, "will exist only if new ministries are conceived and accepted."

To Piveteau, the contemporary Church must find some ways (as did the early Church and the Jewish diaspora) of transmitting and living their faith without recourse to social imposition à la medieval Christendom (pp. 28–9). His four requisites point to how small-church groups might become places of catechesis and discipleship.

Other relevant experiences come from the San Egidio Community. Described by one of its leaders as "both a child of Vatican II and of the 1968 student movement with its strong push for authenticity and its indignation at the dramatic conditions of life of so many people," the Community of San Egidio is an international lay association with more than 15,000 members worldwide (Marazziti 1996, p. 73). It was founded by a group of Italian high school students in 1968 and now operates in two dozen countries (in both First and Third World settings).

While the San Egidio Community is less comprehensive in its practice of community than some other initiatives, it does offer itself as an example of how the two-tiered expectations (minimal for lay persons, more demanding for religious) can be overcome through an intensive practice of life for and with the poor, daily prayer and Scripture study, and solidarity with those ostracized or neglected by affluent groups.

Members of San Egidio combine service and life with the poor, AIDS sufferers, the homeless, or immigrants with daily evening prayer at a common location. Evening prayer is the spiritual sustenance and bonding practice of the community.

> Our prayer is a way of coming face to face with Jesus and finding or refinding ourselves for what we truly are . . . For us, this evening prayer has been and is the great antidote to the violent self-affirmation of oneself; it is the

antidote to an ideological or merely sociological approach to the one who is poor. It is the great antidote to those fastidious forms of "proud humility" or the pathetic sense of superiority which can take root even among Christians. (Marazziti 1996, p. 75)

In building their evening prayer around Scripture, members of San Egidio found "a great freedom from the prevailing ideologies."

The Scriptures liberated us from the ideology which asserted that "every-thing is political," and from the Marxist ideology and from the ideology where everyone withdrew from public life. Scriptures also set us free from the "yuppyism" which came later, and it frees us today from "consumerism" and the temptation to "group" or "ethnic" closure. (Marazziti 1996, p. 75)

In recent years, San Egidio increasingly has found a calling to peace-making in its vocation. The group helped negotiate the settlement of civil war in Mozambique, played a role in negotiating a preliminary peace ac-cord in Guatemala, and has begun peacemaking initiatives regarding Bu-rundi, the Sudan, and Algeria. Its credibility as a mediating/negotiating body comes not from those sources typical of state diplomats but from its commitment to peaceful means and service to the poor (Marazziti 1996, p. 77). In all of this, as in their evangelical commitment to the poor and prayerful formation, San Egidio seeks fidelity "to the whole Gospel, to live with urgency a truly apostolic life as the apostles did." It is the voca-tion of all Christians, whatever their status, "to change the world through the weakness of the Gospel" (Marazziti 1996, p. 74).

As a model for how a lifelong catechumenate might operate, the San Egidio movement combines significant time devoted to Scripture, prayer, and service; it forms small groups built upon consultation and wide-ranging discussion; and it privileges growth in one's identity as a Christian and disciple over the claims of nationalism, class, and ethnic loyalties. Its canonical recognition by the Holy See in 1986 (as an international public lay association) may point less to its domestication than to its dispropor-tionate impact in generating thousands of committed disciples in wildly varied social environments—including in those countries deeply affected by the global culture industries.

Perhaps the most provocative and controversial model with potential relevance for a lifelong catechumenate lies with an already-existing prac-tice of such: the Neocatechumenate Movement. Some information in this section is derived from an overview article and interview published in the early 1990s (see "The Neocatechumenate Movement," n.d.); these documents, as well as a collection of articles opposed to the Neocatechumenate can be found at the website of PASCH (Parishioners Against a Secret Church, http://outworld.compuserve.com/homepages/Ronald_Haynes/).

Founded by two young people in Madrid in 1964, the Neocatechumenate Movement operates on the belief that "the Church must become more of a community and return to the example of the early Christians." Its founders believe that, for most Christians, infant baptism is a seed that lays dormant, nearly dead. It joins these two assumptions in practices of "post-baptismal Christian initiation realized with the methods and forms of the early Church" ("Neocatechumenate Movement," pp. 1–2).

The Neocatechumenate, called "The Way" by its members, received Vatican concessions regarding liturgical practice in 1988: members celebrate the Eucharist with unleavened bread and wine in Masses of more than two hours duration; Scripture readings are followed by the congregants' comments and reflections, which are then worked into the priest's homily; and the Rite of Peace follows the Ambrosian rite. Movement spokespersons claim that young adults in particular (ages 25–50) are attracted to the liturgical vitality evidenced in parishes affected by the Neocatechumenate ("Neocatechumenate Movement," pp. 2–3).

The formative practices of the Neocatechumenate are encountered in several sequential stages, generally over a seven-year period (DiNoia 1996, p. 280). Passage through the stages is not assured: a board of catechists examines candidates, who in turn may appeal negative decisions. The stages can be described as:

1. Kerygma (proclamation), an introductory stage. A parish priest introduces the Neocatechumenate to his parish through preaching by the movement's itinerant catechists. This leads to the formation of catechetical groups of no more than 30–50 persons each.

2. Precatechumenate, or kenosis ("emptying") stage, which focuses on life conversion. Members of the communities meet one evening a week for a gospel service, and for Mass on Saturday evening. Each person spends one Sunday per month alone. This stage, usually lasting two years, ends with the founding catechists returning for a three-day retreat that prepares members for passage to the next stages.

3 and 4. The Catechumenate Stage, itself in two phases. The first focuses community members on study of Scripture, Eucharistic practice, and community life. In this period, members work to make God the cen-

ter of their lives, displacing the modern idols of wealth, career, and the like. The first phase, usually one year in length, again ends with a return of the visiting catechists, who move the communities into the final phase of the Catechumenate process. Intensive individual prayer and reflection typify this stage, which leads members to assume evangelization roles within their families, within the catechetical communities, and within the parish at large. Renewal of baptismal promises marks the final formal stage of the Neocatechumenate.

5. The formal catechetical process complete, groups dedicate themselves to lives of service in the parish or in missionary endeavors ("Neocatechumenate Movement," pp. 1–2).

Since its founding, the movement claims to have created more than 13,500 communities in 4,000 parishes (themselves distributed across 780 dioceses in more than 90 countries)("Neocatechumenate Movement," p. 1). Another source offers more modest numbers, of 10,000 communities in 3,000 parishes, and more than 200,000 members as of 1990 (DiNoia 1996, pp. 280–1). More than 1,000 parishes in Italy have introduced the Neocatechumenate, and the movement has begun providing mission training to diocesan priests in Neocatechumenate seminaries in several countries.

Criticisms of the Neocatechumenate are numerous and are of several types. Traditionalist groups opposed to the reforms of Vatican II find the movement's liturgical style to be too radical; doctrinally, these groups claim the movement's founders underplay doctrines of priestly absolution and the Real Presence in the Eucharist. A second sort of criticism accuses the movement of creating a "Church within the Church," undermining diocesan structures and authorities and engaging in separatist practices. A third objection finds the movement to be cult-like in nature, compared to the Unification Church ("Moonies") (see PASCH documents). The Diocese of Clifton (U.K.) is among many to have investigated the movement's activities in its parishes and has found them to have undermined parish unity and vitality (PASCH documents). Finally, having once been investigated by the Holy Office on suspicions of doctrinal, hermeneutic, and pastoral deviation, the movement in 1986 received a personal delegate from Pope John Paul II to act as intermediary between the movement and various Vatican offices. One may ask whether the Neocatechumenate has been enlisted in the Pope's project of authoritarian centralization in a way similar to Opus Dei, another movement founded by Spaniards and accused of divisive, cult-like (but, unlike the Neocatechumenate, ultra-orthodox) practices.

I am not troubled by the traditionalist objections to the Neocatechumenate initiative, and I am not surprised that bishops in some locales would be troubled by the presence of energized lay groups outside their direct control. I am more concerned by the accusation of cult-like tendencies, although I am aware of how easily such accusations have been thrown against legitimate church renewal movements in the past; at a minimum, more information is needed. It would be disappointing, but not altogether novel, if a lay-based revitalization initiative were co-opted by the centralizing ambitions of the Vatican, although I defer to those more knowledgeable as to whether the history of the Neocatechumenate fits the description (or whether, like Opus Dei for instance, reinforcing papal power was among its founding ambitions).

For me, after all, the point is not whether the Neocatechumenate Movement is to be defended, but whether it has something valid to teach regarding the formation of lay Christians. Like the San Egidio experience and Piveteau's overview, the Neocatechumenate engages people's time and attention in the sustained development of Christian practices and capabilities through prayer, study, worship, and service. Like the other examples, it points toward ways of religious formation focused on adults, not just children, while underscoring the countercultural nature of the gospel and the life of discipleship.

One could point toward other examples of Christian formation aimed at adults on a long-term basis: the various pastoral initiatives identified by Michael Warren (1997); the Brotherhood of the Common Life, an important late medieval movement that sought to bring the zeal (although not the forms) of early monasticism into the lives of lay believers, and as such was an important antecedent to formation-based innovations in the Protestant and Catholic Reformations (Fuller 1995); the Catholic Worker movement and its offspring; and some of the small faith groups, intentional communities, and base communities described by Wuthnow (1994) and others, although the heterogeneity of such groups is ignored at one's peril (see Levine 1992). Whatever the forms, and with more experiments and variations being better than fewer, some sort of means of "converting the baptized" is needed if the church hopes to live up to the mandates of the gospel in hypermediated cultures. A period of "media-detoxification" might also be involved in a lifelong catechumenate program; filling at least some of the dozens of hours per week spent watching television for church-centered prayer/study/action would be far superior to a "just turn it off" approach that failed to substitute formative practices for the culture industries. Such a detoxification period might help people perceive anew the cultural vectors that shape our world and may help us to see the taken-for-granted culture industries as the strange, enveloping phenomena they are.

Liturgy and Catechesis

Another desirable set of changes in church practices and discourse regarding formation involves liturgical matters. The Church needs to reaffirm the close ties between liturgy and catechesis. As noted by Harmon Smith:

> Liturgy both reflects and teaches us the kinds of people we are and are meant to be. It is both catechesis and celebration. And it is the divorce of these two, their separation into virtually vacuum-sealed compartments, which is liturgy's (and the church's) undoing. (Smith 1995, p. *x*)

According to Warren:

> The only decisive counter-force to the cultural pressures of our time may be the power of whole communities struggling together toward an appropriate spirituality characterized by a transformed way of paying attention. These communities will be formed with the collaboration of liturgists and catechists.
>
> An important task in liturgical-catechetical collaboration in an image-dominated culture is that of becoming more aware of images and how they work . . . The deeper problem is not [merely] that we look at images ceaselessly. The deeper problem is that we look at reality through images.
>
> Catechists and liturgists alike need to explore more consciously the power-laden metaphors proclaimed in our catechesis and dramatized in our worship. We can too easily sidestep the radical, culture-questioning images and substitute slicker, more easily acceptable ones. (Warren 1989, pp. 77–8, 82)

Making explicit the connections between catechesis and liturgy also requires expanding our understanding of the nature of worship. Walter Brueggemann returns our attention to the "work of the people" in liturgy, which is "to process shared experience through the normative narratives, images, metaphors, and symbols of the community" (1988, p. 30). For liturgy to mediate "energy, power, authority, assurance, and mandate" to Christians, it must not be a remembering but a new enactment of the claims of the good news in our day. "The liturgic act is the moment of announcement in which old claims are made present realities, in which victories won in other places are made available as victories in this place now. Through such speech the world is changed" (1988, pp. 34–5, 36).

Seen in this way, as part of a transformative enactment that shapes a people along the lines of biblical narratives and struggles, worship can lead us "to a dangerous and exciting place, a place where calculation withers and imagination blooms" (Webber and Clapp 1988, p. 82). As a further expression of the Church as "vision clinic," liturgical construction of alternative ways of seeing and living must be acknowledged as a radical, even subversive part of the church's character. As noted by Brueggemann,

> the life-world created in biblical worship is one among many theoretical worlds, and therefore such worship is not only constitutive, but inevitably polemical. Praise insists not only that this is the true world, but that other worlds are false. World-creation also includes world-delegitimation of other worlds. The Church sings praises not only toward God but against other gods. (Brueggemann 1988, p. 27)

To Smith, the Christian life can be described as learning "to see *everything* within the interpretive frame of Jesus' life, ministry, death, resurrection, and ascension—that is, to see with the eyes of faith." That Jesus' ministry focused so much on blindness (physical and ideological) and its correction suggests that "*any other way* of seeing ourselves and the world is wrong, mistaken, not true, or is, as he suggests . . . a confusion of sight with blindness" (Smith 1995, p. 27).

The paradox of liturgy, of course, is that its capacity to transform Christian communities and persons is elusive and resists crude manipulation—it is not a "tool" to be utilized in a mechanistic fashion. As noted by Webber and Clapp:

> Worship cannot be reduced to psychotherapy or political consciousness-raising. It is first and foremost the service of God and needs no other justification. The transformation of worshipers is not its central aim. In fact, we are not apt to be changed by worship if we come to it primarily to be changed, for then we will be back to concentrating on ourselves. The transformation of the church is a by-product of the liturgy. It occurs only when the church is determined foremost simply to worship God. (Webber and Clapp 1988, pp. 69–70)

This paradox is real, and confronting it is an urgent matter. Just as global culture industries have rendered catechesis more difficult and more necessary, so have they impacted negatively on liturgical practices and expectations. Susan White's important study of the transformation of liturgy by technology and rationalization includes some urgent cautions on this matter. She extends some of the concerns of Mark Searle, who writes:

> We tend to think too much of what the church might bring to society and too little of what society is already bringing to the church. We enthuse about what new prayers and new liturgical music might do to shape the liturgical assembly, overlooking the fact that culture has gotten there before us, unconsciously shaping the attitudes and language of both the experts and the participants. (Searle, quoted in White 1994, p. 39)

For her part, White notes the impact of consumerism on liturgy and the expectations of (mostly passive) worshipers. "For most participants, worship is judged by its ability to uplift, inspire, and console. But its success at accomplishing those things is highly dependent upon its conformity to other elements of the technological environment," among which she lists short attention spans, the desire for stimulation of several senses at once, a quick pace, entertainment features, and high-quality music and production values (1994, p. 118).

To her, the big question is:

> To what extent should Christian worship be created and understood as a countercultural force, an activity that calls into question the values and presuppositions of the age of technology, and to what extent should it conform to the kinds of contemporary expectations that the prevalence of technologies fosters? It is just possible the very survival of Christian worship as a form of religious expression depends upon the answer. (White 1994, p. 120)

Justice and Social Engagement

Just as lifelong catechesis remains weak when divorced from liturgy, so do liturgy and formation require consideration of social engagement and justice when constructing a discourse/practice appropriate to a discipleship-based church.

While catechesis and liturgy may seem far removed from "real" politics and social justice efforts (lobbying legislatures, supporting candidates, and similar efforts to impact state action), discipleship-based ecclesiology has its own "politics," and presupposes a commitment to the social demands of the gospel. What differs, of course, are definitions of politics, questions of ends and means, and short-term versus long-term horizons. And while mainstream theologians excoriate tight-ecclesiology thinkers for not being socially "responsible" or helping the poor via the political process, I am unpersuaded of the moral or practical superiority of existing arrangements. Were the Catholic tradition more than an incidental identity for the 52 million nominal Catholics in the United States, for example, we would almost surely see less privation, more sharing of resources and efforts, and a more critical stance regarding the regnant systems of racial, economic, and gendered preference.

Existing practices of mainstream Christian formation (Protestant and Catholic) have had surprisingly little impact on attitudes and practices (and "politics") regarding wealth and acquisitiveness, according to Princeton sociologist Robert Wuthnow. In most U.S. churches, says Wuthnow, "what religious faith does more clearly than anything else is to add a dollop of piety to the materialistic amalgam in which most of us live" (1993, p. 240). So perhaps I will be forgiven for not being overly impressed by the social justice claims of minimalistic Christianity; if it is true that "by their fruits you shall know them," then I don't find these fruits so uncontroversially superior as to disqualify other efforts to cultivate the gospel.

Constructing discourse and practices based on the church-as-polis is not an apolitical process, after all, not a withdrawal from the "real" world, and not an abandonment of those outside the Christian fold. It *is* different from what is referred to as "social responsibility" in mainline churches, on several levels.

I have already commented on the state-centered nature of politics in the modernist worldview and the depth of mainstream Christianity's identification of "politics" with "what states do." What states "do," I suggest, is exercise lethal force in the pursuit of various objectives—order, justice, prosperity, self-preservation, elite security, and the like. States vary in their internal structures and dynamics (more or less authoritarian, more or less participatory), but none of them are—or can be—nonviolent. Pax Romana, or Pax Americana, or any other kind of peace purchased by state power, is one in which killing for some social good is legitimate and inevitable. One's goals in politics may target something other than the direct administration of lethal means (helping the poor as opposed to running the military or police, for example), but the former ultimately depends upon the presence and actions of the latter.

Like Hauerwas, Yoder, and other advocates of a more radical ecclesiology (I would include the Catholic Worker and Berrigan-inspired movements here), I am convinced that pacifism is an irremovable part of a discipleship-based Christianity. I can find no intellectually or theologically persuasive move that puts the sword in Jesus' hand or that allows us to disregard Jesus' pacifism as normative for his disciples. Unlike Yoder and Hauerwas (but like the Catholic Worker/Berrigan tradition), I maintain that Christian pacifism is incompatible with voting, holding state office, and other direct state-supportive practices (e.g., see Cartwright 1994, p. 8; Hauerwas and Willimon 1996a, p. 115). Given these differences, what we agree on is a rejection of the politics of Caiaphas and his successors, to whom "it is better that one man die than the whole community" (Jn 11:50; 18:14).

The charge that discipleship-based Christianity ignores political responsibilities, therefore, privileges a notion of "politics" incompatible with the practices and example of Jesus. As John Howard Yoder notes, calls to act "responsibly" in the world as citizens requires accepting

> a specific body of alternative wisdom marked by the fact that it not only comes from somewhere else than Jesus but also, necessarily, tells us to do something other than what Jesus tells his disciples to do. Jesus tells us to love our enemies, including holding their lives sacred. The orders of creation, known through the specific locations of some of us in civil responsibility, tell us that for the sake of our love for the life of some nearer neighbor we might need to destroy the enemy neighbor. Jesus tells us to share our bread and our money: those of us who have the particular calling of entrepreneur or of banker should do just the opposite, because there is a structure in the order of things that declares certain spheres to be independent of the pertinence of the instructions of Jesus . . . [In this, all that remains is] to haggle with "realism" to determine how much obedience [to Jesus] we can get away with. (Yoder 1994, p. 123)

Questions of ends, of legitimate and illegitimate means, are unavoidable when considering the obligations of churches centered on the life and practices of Jesus. Processes of formation with this center, I contend, should have real-world effects on lifestyle, vocation, and service that take things like the "option for the poor" more seriously than they are under present arrangements.

Radical ecclesiology implies a politics and ministry that reach beyond intrachurch concerns and into the wider world; formation, after all, constructs a people capable of taking the good news from the church to the world. When done properly, the process can lead to catechists and agents of formation being seen as "subversive" and "dangerous" by states and other agents of exploitative order (see Warren 1989, pp. 69–70). Catechesis done as apprenticeship to Jesus involves joining spirituality and lifestyle, a politically charged connection in any era. On this point, Warren's insights are valuable:

> The challenge of finding an appropriate spirituality is partly the challenge of finding an appropriate lifestyle. Second, the crisis of the human spirit in our time [and place] is the crisis of knowing what things are worth paying attention to. For a follower of Jesus, the discipline of spirituality in our time must be the discipline, not so much of praying effectively, as of paying attention to the proper matters. (Warren 1989, p. 88)

The spirituality that disciples of Jesus seek is different from what Warren calls "lower-case spirituality"—the (mostly unexamined) commitments, hopes, choices, uses of time, and the like that everyone has, often derived from the dominant culture. Discipleship requires an "upper-case spirituality," which "involves an active, disciplined search for God, the result of a religious transformation seen as a gifted act of God." In this view, "spirituality is a *systematic* way of attending to the presence of God" (1989, p. 90).

Christian spirituality—of the upper-case variety—becomes a politically relevant phenomenon when it affects the church members' life structure—where we spend and how we earn our resources, with whom we talk, what we read, how much television we watch, with whom we share, and so on (Warren 1989, pp. 96–7). It partakes not of the surface politics of state action and domination but of what Webber and Clapp describe as "depth politics." The latter "forms visions and identities . . . the way people see the world and understand their purpose in it" (1988, p. 12). While this sort of praxis will seem irresponsibly slow in a world that demands instant justice and instant "solutions" to problems, it may reflect a more sober appraisal of the lack of power held by Christian communities—unless, of course, they deny their vocation and accept the ways of the earthly kingdoms (an offer extended to, but refused by, Jesus in Mt 4:8–11; Lk 4:5–8).

Like it or not, Christians do not have unlimited choice of means to do good in the world—we cannot eradicate poverty by killing off the poor, nor are we allowed to protect the ecosystem by deliberately starving "excess" people. Jesus himself eschewed many instrumentally "effective" means in advancing the kingdom (Lk 4:9–12; Mt 26:51–53), choosing instead courses of action that engaged the imagination, demonstrated new possibilities, and subverted the presumed dominion of death. A culture blinded by sensory and symbolic overload will struggle with politics as symbolic, expressive, and evocative; it nonetheless reflects the way of Jesus. As Yoder notes:

> When Jesus washed the feet of his disciples he made no abiding contribution to the hygiene of Palestine. Nevertheless, this act took a position in the world that has in itself both spiritual and ethical value. Similarly, when Christians devote themselves to the care of the seriously ill or the mentally retarded, of the unproductive aged, the fruitfulness of their service cannot be measured by any statistical index of economic efficiency. (Yoder 1994, p. 204)

If the politics of discipleship seems an elusive notion to many, its political significance has not been lost on some secular powerholders who have encountered variations of it in parts of Latin America, the Philippines, and elsewhere. Christians become subversive when they deny the readings of "reality" preferred by existing powerholders, when they refuse allegiance to the lesser idols of state, class, or lineage. Were the death squads of the 1980s to have focused only on the "political" Christians (those seeking control of the state) we would have seen far fewer catechists tortured, murdered, and disappeared. State actors often have a wider view of politics than do church people who are oblivious to the legitimating/delegitimating practices of formation, worship, and discipleship.

At the extreme, one can see the power (long-term, non-Constantinian) of formation and liturgy to influence social action and the prophetic confrontation of oppression in a recent work by Anna Peterson. Her article, "Religious Narratives and Political Protest," explains that for some people in El Salvador,

> the story of Jesus' life, death, and resurrection provides a lens through which to make sense of the times through which they have lived . . . This meaning

relies upon a conviction that they are indeed living "in the times of the Romans"—that their experiences echo and in fact re-enact the events of sacred history. [These believers] place their own lives in the context of an encompassing narrative of faith, persecution, and ultimate reward, intertwining real and sacred history. (Peterson 1996, pp. 26–7)

These embodied religious narratives, learned and internalized through strong ecclesial structures and experiences, impact "politically" (understood broadly) in three ways, according to Peterson. First, they help form a common identity among persons that situates individuality within a larger community (p. 30). In my terms, such narratives privilege members' identities as followers of Jesus above competing identities. Second, religious narratives can inspire heroic, often risky, action in pursuit of the goals of the Kingdom. Third, these narratives offer a utopian or alternative vision of the future, which (when resonating with people's understanding of their past) "enlarges" their view of the future's possibilities (pp. 30–1). In other words, persons choosing to live through the narratives and priorities of Jesus often engaged in sustained, prophetic, and delegitimating actions in ways that would seem "unrealistic" or "imprudent" in secular terms. They further dared to critique the present by comparisons to a promised-but-delayed future Kingdom of God—hardly part of policy analysis in the running of a modern state.

Peterson does not suggest that poor Christians in El Salvador "adopted" these narratives in order to increase their political clout or to gain an edge in movement-formation; indeed, she recognizes the degree to which conventional interest-based theories of social mobilization run aground on such narrative-inspired practices (pp. 41–2). And although not every situation is as extreme as El Salvador in the 1970s and 1980s and not every Christian community will live the core narratives in the same way, the choice of a church—any church—to practice a discipleship model of the faith is also to practice a type of politics that is often unintelligible, offensive, or threatening to existing structures of political, economic, and social power. A church-as-polis, or countercultural, model need not attempt to seize the state to implement the preferential option for the poor; but the preferential option for the poor, if made central and not peripheral to church practices of lifelong catechesis and worship, may become a more subversive, substantive, and prophetic practice of the good news than it has been thus far. By refusing to accede to political realism's diminution of politics to "the art of the possible" (defined usually by state-centric criteria), ecclesially based practices of justice, forgiveness, and charity themselves become a politics:

> The church is a political alternative to the world when [for example] the members of a base community share their food, visit the sick, build a well, or defy government tanks to demand an end to torture.
>
> To see the world clearly for what it is, Christians must create communities that are not-world, communities where the gospel story is enacted without regard for political expedience. As the testimony of many persecuted members of base communities can affirm, however, the very process of forming such communities is a highly subversive, and therefore political, act. (Cavanaugh 1994, pp. 77, 81)

Concluding Thoughts

I am aware that this last chapter has ventured away from discussions of advertising and television, Time-Warner and Disney. I have done so because, as I suggest at the outset of this chapter, the problems created for the church by global culture industries cannot be addressed using the tools of those industries nor via religious education as presently practiced. The only plausible—but not guaranteed effective—recourse is a church-centered one: only those that enlarge the claims of the gospel in the lives of Christians have much hope of diminishing the claims of the commercial orchestrators of attention.

And although I am no expert in pastoral practice, I have attempted to offer some food for thought for whomever might pick up the challenges I have outlined. Demonstrating the breadth of my limitations will have been worthwhile if other men and women committed to the "politics of Jesus" are inspired to offer better efforts in response to my own.

Considered together, the sorts of changes in church practice, self-definition, and discourse I recommend may put the Church in a better place to resist the negative influences of the global culture industries. Although there are no guarantees or automatic progressions here, I would hope that building the Church as an alternative community in the world would have several effects:

1. More time spent learning and living the language and habits of the gospel and the church;

2. Less time spent consuming and interacting with the products of commercial culture industries;

3. The previous two, taken together, might provide Christians with greater distance from the culture industries and the consumerist worldview upon which they depend;

4. An enhanced capacity not only to see through and denounce existing unjust relations of power, but to experiment with practices, programs, and commitments that demonstrate possibilities for life together that confound conventional assumptions regarding the centrality of violence, greed, and dominative power in ordering human affairs.

I am not so foolish that I imagine that global culture industries present the only, or the most immediate, threat to the church and the gospel. But the patterns and interactions I have identified here deserve attention precisely because their import is not immediately or obviously apparent. They are important, they are likely to intensify, and the negative effects will outweigh the positive.

As I was finishing this final chapter, the Walt Disney Corporation named a new member of its Board of Directors. Chairman Michael Eisner announced the appointment of Father Leo O'Donovan, S.J., President of Georgetown University. According to Eisner, O'Donovan was chosen not only for his moral leadership, but especially for his business acumen and managerial success at the Jesuit institution. The Mouse marches onward.

References

Advertising Age. 1995. Facts and Figures/Vital Statistics. Available from http://www.adage.com

_____ 1992a. Vatican taps Well Comm for ads. Dec. 7, p. 8.

_____ 1992b. Global News. Nov. 2, p. 8.

Aetatis Novae. 1992. Pontifical Council for Social Communication. *Origins* 21:42.

Aglietta, Michel. 1979. *A Theory of Capitalist Regulation.* London: NLB Books.

American Demographics. 1994. The 1994 Directory/International.

Amin, Ash. 1994. Post-Fordism: Models, fantasies, and phantoms of transition. In *Post-Fordism,* ed. Ash Amin. Oxford: Blackwell.

Amin, Samir. 1977. Self-reliance and the new international economic order. *Monthly Review* 29:3.

Apple, Michael. 1990. *Ideology and Curriculum.* London: Routledge.

Arthur, Chris. 1995. Meaning, media, and religion [review essay]. *Religious Studies Review* 21:2.

Asad, Talal. 1993. *Genealogies of Religion: Discipline and Reasons of Power in Christianity and Islam.* Baltimore: Johns Hopkins University Press.

Audiovisual media education: An urgent social concern. 1995. *Media Development,* no. 2.

Barnet, Richard, and John Cavanagh. 1994. *Global Dreams.* New York: Simon & Schuster.

Belk, Russell, Melanie Wallendorf, and John Sherry. 1989. The sacred and the profane in consumer behavior: Theodicy on the odyssey. *Journal of Consumer Research* 16.

Belk, Russell, and Nan Zhou. 1986. Learning to want things. *Advances in Consumer Research* 14.

Bellah, Robert, Richard Madsen, William Sullivan, Ann Swidler, and Steven Tipton. 1985. *Habits of the Heart.* Berkeley: University of California Press.

Berger, Peter. 1986. *The Capitalist Revolution: Fifty Propositions About Prosperity, Equality, & Liberty.* New York: Basic Books.

Bernstein, Richard J. 1971. *Praxis and Action.* Philadelphia: University of Pennsylvania Press.

Biernatzki, W. E. 1993. Negative to positive for a religious perspective among media professionals. *Communication Research Trends* 13:2, Part 2.

Bloomberg Business News. 1994. TV seen as medium to get message to Chinese public. *Chicago Tribune,* Jan. 24, p. 4, sec. 4.

Boff, Leonardo. 1978. *Jesus Christ Liberator.* Maryknoll, N.Y.: Orbis Books.

Boomershine, Thomas E. 1987. Religious education and media change: A historical sketch. *Religious Education* 82:2.

Boyack, Kenneth, ed. 1992. *The New Catholic Evangelization.* New York: Paulist Press.

Brockelman, Paul. 1992. *The Inside Story: A Narrative Approach to Religious Understanding and Truth.* Albany, N.Y.: SUNY Press.

Brueggemann, Walter. 1995. Preaching as reimagination. *Theology Today* 52:3.

———— 1988. *Israel's Praise: Doxology Against Idolatry and Ideology.* Philadelphia: Fortress Press.

———— 1982. *The Creative Word: Canon as a Model for Biblical Education.* Philadelphia: Fortress.

Buckley, James J. 1992. *Seeking the Humanity of God: Practices, Doctrines, and Catholic Theology.* Collegeville, Minn.: The Liturgical Press.

Budde, Michael. 1992. *The Two Churches: Catholicism & Capitalism in the World System.* Durham, N.C.: Duke University Press.

Butkus, Russell A. 1987. Dangerous memory and social justice education. *Religious Education* 82:3.

Campbell, David. 1992. *Writing Security.* Minneapolis: University of Minnesota Press.

Cartwright, Michael. 1994. Radical reform, radical Catholicity: John Howard Yoder's vision of the faithful church. Foreword to J. H. Yoder, *The Royal Priesthood: Essays Ecclesiological and Ecumenical.* Grand Rapids, Mich.: Eerdmans.

Castelli, James, and Joseph Gremillion. 1987. *The Emerging Parish: The Notre Dame Study of Catholic Life Since Vatican II.* New York: Harper and Row.

Cavanaugh, William T. 1994. The ecclesiologies of Medellin and the lessons of the base communities. *Cross Currents,* Spring.

Celio, Mary Beth. 1993. Catholics: Who, how many, and where? *America,* Jan. 9.

Charry, Ellen T. 1994. Raising Christian children in a pagan culture. *Christian Century,* Feb. 16.

Chase-Dunn, Christopher. 1994. Technology and the logic of world-systems. In *Transcending the State-Global Divide,* eds. R. Palan and B. Gills. Boulder: Lynne Rienner.

———— 1989. *Global Formation: Structures of the World-Economy.* Cambridge: Blackwell.

Clark, Douglas Kent. 1994. The catechism: Instruction for discipleship. *Church,* Winter.

Clifton diocesan Neo-Catechumenate enquiry. (http:www.tasc.ac.uk/cc/briefing/9601/s006.htm).

Coleman, John, and Miklos Tomka, eds. 1993. *Mass Media. Concilium,* no. 6.

Colson, Charles, and Ellen Santilli Vaughn. 1992. Welcome to McChurch. *Christianity Today*, Nov. 23.

Communio et Progressio. 1971. Pontifical Commission for Social Communication. *Origins* 1:44.

Conference on "Religion, Television, and the Information Superhighway." 1994. *Media Development*, no. 4.

Cook, William A. 1992. Here's to Europe 1992 and global glue. *Journal of Advertising Research*, Jan.-Feb.

Cox, Harvey. 1973. *The Seduction of the Spirit: The Use and Misuse of People's Religion.* New York: Simon and Schuster.

Crawford, Marisa, and Graham Rossiter. 1995. The spiritual formation of young Catholics through religious education. *The Living Light* 31:4.

Cuddihy, John Murray. 1978. *No Offense: Civil Religion and Protestant Taste.* New York: Seabury.

Cutler, Blayne. 1989. Third world marketing. *American Demographics* 11:16.

Denman, Ann McKinstry. 1992. C.C.D.: "Central City Dump"? *America*, Oct. 3.

Der Derian, James. 1992. *Antidiplomacy.* Cambridge: Blackwell.

DiNoia, J. A. 1996. Neocatechumenal way. *New Catholic Encyclopedia*, Supplement 1989–95.

———. 1992. *The Diversity of Religions.* Washington, D.C.: Catholic University of America Press.

———. 1990. Varieties of religious aims: Beyond exclusivism, inclusivism, and pluralism. In *Theology and Dialogue: Essays in Conversation with George Lindbeck*, ed. Bruce Marshall. South Bend, Ind.: University of Notre Dame Press.

Donovan, Vincent. 1992. Refounding church: A paradigm shift. *Chicago Studies* 31:2.

Downey, Michael. 1992. Hurdles to the holy: Cultural obstacles to prayer. *Chicago Studies* 31:1.

Driver, Tom F. 1987. Theology of culture. *Religious Education* 82:2.

Duggan, Robert. 1994. Taking on a new identity. *Catholic World* 237:1419.

Dulles, Avery. 1982. *A Church To Believe In: Discipleship and the Dynamics of Freedom.* New York: Crossroads.

———. 1974. *Models of the Church.* New York: Image Books.

Dumestre, Marcel. 1995. Postfundamentalism and the Christian intentional learning community. *Religious Education* 90:2.

———. 1994. Moving beyond fundamentalism: Religious education for adult spirituality. *Catholic World* 237:1421.

———. 1993. Toward effective adult religious education. *Origins*, May 27.

Ecumenical News International (ENI). 1995a. Vatican Radio hopes to sell a million CDs featuring the pope. *ENI Bulletin*, no. 19.

———. 1995b. Surprise! Advertisements take the cross out of Easter. *ENI Bulletin*, Mar. 28.

Eipers, Carole. 1994. Adolescent faith development: Facing the tough questions. *Catholic World* 237:1421.

Ekstrom, Reynolds R. 1992. Consumerism and youth. In *Media and Culture,* ed. Reynolds R. Ekstrom. New Rochelle, N.Y.: Don Bosco/Multimedia.

Elam, Mark. 1994. Puzzling out the post-Fordist debate: Technology, markets, and institutions. In *Post-Fordism,* ed. Ash Amin. Oxford: Blackwell.

Elias, John. 1989. Adult religious education: An analysis of Roman Catholic documents published in Australia, Canada, England and Wales, and the United States. *Religious Education* 84:1.

Elkin, Carolyn. 1993. Religious education's power to nurture faith. *Origins,* May 27.

Engel, James F. 1993. Will the great commission become the great ad campaign? *Christianity Today,* Apr. 26.

_____ 1992. The great commission advertising campaign: Misuse of the mass media in world evangelization. *Transformation* 9, Oct.-Dec.

Enloe, Cynthia. 1993. *The Morning After.* Berkeley: University of California Press.

_____ 1990. *Bananas, Beaches, and Bases: Making Feminist Sense of International Politics.* Berkeley: University of California Press.

Evangelii Nuntiandi. 1975. Available from (http://listserv.american.edu/catholic/church/papal/paulvi/p6evang.txt).

Evans, Peter. 1979. *Dependent Development: The Alliance of Multinational, State, and Local Capital in Brazil.* Princeton: Princeton University Press.

Ewen, Stuart. 1988. *All Consuming Images: The Politics of Style in Contemporary Culture.* New York: Basic Books.

Firat, A. Fuat. 1991. The consumer in postmodernity. *Advances in Consumer Research,* no. 18.

Fitzgerald, Mark. 1989. The Catholic press. *Editor & Publisher,* May 6.

Foley, John. 1994. Basic training needed in use of communications media. *L'Osservatore Romano,* Oct. 19, pp. 5–6.

Fore, William F. 1994. Commercial media versus cultural and spiritual values. *Media Development,* no. 3.

_____ 1990. *Mythmakers: Gospel, Culture, and the Media.* New York: Friendship Press.

_____ 1987. A theology of communication. *Religious Education* 82:2.

Foucault, Michel. 1980. *Power/Knowledge.* New York: Pantheon.

_____ 1979. *Discipline and Punish: The Birth of the Prison.* New York: Vintage.

Fox, Richard Wrightman, and T. J. Jackson Lears, eds. 1983. *The Culture of Consumption: Critical Essays in American History.* New York: Pantheon.

Frank, Tom. 1995. Dark age: Why Johnny can't dissent. *The Baffler,* no. 6.

Frantz, Nadine Pence. 1994. Biblical interpretation in a "non-sense" world: Text, revelation, and interpretive community. *Brethren Life and Thought,* no. 49.

Frei, Hans. 1974. *The Eclipse of Biblical Narrative.* New Haven: Yale University Press.

Fuller, Ross. 1995. *The Brotherhood of the Common Life and Its Influence.* Albany, N.Y.: SUNY Press.

Gabriel, Trip. 1995. MTV-inspired images, but the message for children is a moral one. *New York Times,* Apr. 16, p. 12.

Galbraith, John Kenneth. 1958. *The Affluent Society.* Boston: Houghton Mifflin.

Gallup, George, Jr., and Jim Castelli. 1987. *The American Catholic People.* Garden City, N.J.: Doubleday.

Gandy, Oscar H., Jr. 1993. *The Panoptic Sort: A Political Economy of Personal Information.* Boulder: Westview Press.

Garvey, John. 1994. An alienating culture. *Commonweal,* Nov. 18.

Gibeau, Dawn. 1994. Catholic education groups collaborate on what to teach and in what manner. *National Catholic Reporter,* July 29.

Gill, Robin. 1995. Moral communities and Christian ethics. *Studies in Christian Ethics* 8:1.

Giroux, Henry, and Peter McLaren, eds. 1989. *Critical Pedagogy, the State, and Cultural Struggle.* Albany, N.Y.: SUNY Press.

Goerne, Carrie. 1992. "Research sonar" takes a sounding of subconscious buying decisions. *Marketing News,* June 8.

Goethals, Gregor. 1991. The electronic golden calf. In *Video Icons and Values,* eds. A. Olson, C. Parr, and D. Parr. Albany, N.Y.: SUNY Press.

_____ 1990. *The Electronic Golden Calf: Images, Religion, and the Making of Meaning.* Cambridge, Mass.: Cowley Publications.

_____ 1981. *The TV Ritual: Worship at the Video Altar.* Boston: Beacon Press.

Goldman, Ari. 1994. The marketing of the pope. *New York Times,* Aug. 27.

_____ 1993. Questions of censorship shadow Catholic paper. *New York Times,* May 19.

Goll, Sally D. 1994. China serves up bigger rice bowl for ad agencies. *Wall Street Journal,* May 6, p. B5-A.

Gonzalez, David. 1993. Catholic schools enter new age of fundraising, corporate-style. *New York Times,* June 21.

Gramsci, Antonio. 1971. *Selections from the Prison Notebooks.* New York: International Publishers.

Granfield, Patrick, ed. 1994. *The Church and Communication.* Kansas City: Sheed & Ward.

Greeley, Andrew. 1993. Religion not dying out around the world. *Origins* 23:4.

Greeley, Andrew, and William McManus. 1987. *Catholic Contributions: Sociology and Policy.* Chicago: Thomas More Press.

Grey, Mary. 1994. Liberation theology and the bearers of dangerous memory. *New Blackfriars* 75:887.

Haight, Roger. 1994. The church as locus of theology. *Concilium*, no. 6.

———. 1992. On systematic ecclesiology. *Toronto Journal of Theology* 8:2.

Hall, Douglas John. 1992. Ecclesia crucis: The disciple community and the future of the church in North America. *Union Seminary Quarterly Review* 46:1–2.

Hamelink, Kees J. 1983. *Finance and Information: A Study of Converging Interests.* Norwood, N.J.: Ablex.

Hanson, Eric O. 1987. *The Catholic Church and World Politics.* Princeton: Princeton University Press.

Hanvey, James. 1994. Educating for the Kingdom. *The Month*, April.

Hargrove, Barbara. 1987. Theology, education, and the electronic media. *Religious Education* 82:2.

Harvey, David. 1989. *The Condition of Postmodernity: An Enquiry into the Origins of Cultural Change.* Oxford: Blackwell.

Hauerwas, Stanley. 1995a. What could it mean for the church to be Christ's body? *Scottish Journal of Theology* 48:1.

———. 1995b. *In Good Company: The Church as Polis.* South Bend, Ind.: University of Notre Dame Press.

———. 1994a. Whose church? Which future? Whither the Anabaptist vision? *Brethren Life and Thought*, no. 39.

———. 1994b. *Dispatches from the Front.* Durham, N.C.: Duke University Press.

———. 1993. *Unleashing the Scripture: Freeing the Bible from Captivity to America.* Nashville, Tenn.: Abingdon Press.

———. 1988. *Christian Existence Today.* Durham, N.C.: Labyrinth Press.

———. 1981. *A Community of Character.* South Bend, Ind.: University of Notre Dame Press.

Hauerwas, Stanley, and L. Gregory Jones. 1989. Introduction to *Why Narrative? Readings in Narrative Theology.* Grand Rapids, Mich.: Eerdmans.

Hauerwas, Stanley, and William Willimon. 1996a. *Where Resident Aliens Live: Exercises for Christian Practice.* Nashville, Tenn.: Abingdon.

———. 1996b. Your kingdom come. *Sojourners*, May–June.

Hauerwas, Stanley, Nancey Murphy, and Mark Nation, eds. 1994. *Theology Without Foundations: Religious Practice and the Future of Theological Truth.* Nashville, Tenn.: Abingdon.

Heckler-Feltz, Cheryl. 1993. Chaplains become big business. *National Catholic Reporter*, Aug. 13.

Herberg, Will. 1955. *Protestant, Catholic, Jew.* New York: Harper and Row.

Higgins, Gregory C. 1989. The significance of postliberalism for religious education. *Religious Education* 84:1.

Hilliard, Robert L., and Michael C. Keith. 1996. *Global Broadcasting Systems.* Boston: Focal Press.

Hills, Jill. 1994. Dependency theory and its relevance today: International institutions in telecommunications and structural power. *Review of International Studies*, no. 20.

Hobbs, Renée. 1991. Television and the shaping of cognitive skills. In *Video Icons and Values*, eds. A. Olson, C. Parr and D. Parr. Albany, N.Y.: SUNY Press.

Hoffman, Virginia. 1992. Birthing the church. *Chicago Studies* 31:2.

Holt, John. 1981 *Teach Your Own.* New York: Delta.

Horkheimer, Max, and Theodor Adorno. 1944/1994. *The Dialectic of Enlightenment.* New York: Continuum.

Hoy, Daniel Couzens. 1986. Introduction to *Foucault: A Critical Reader,* ed. D. C. Hoy. Oxford: Blackwell.

Hughes, Janice. 1994. The changing multimedia landscape. *Media Studies Journal* 8:1.

Inter Mirifica. 1963. Decree on the means of social communication. Available from (http://www.christusrex.org/www1/CDHN/v12html).

Jacobson, Michael, and Laurie Ann Mazur. 1995. *Marketing Madness: A Survival Guide for a Consumer Society.* Boulder: Westview Press.

Jameson, Frederic. 1991. *Postmodernism: Or the Cultural Logic of Late Capitalism.* Durham, N.C.: Duke University Press.

Janofsky, Michael. 1993. In defense of the pope's brand name. *New York Times,* June 14.

Jeffries, Rosemary. 1992. Media for the sake of the gospel. In *The New Catholic Evangelization,* ed. Kenneth Boyack. New York: Paulist Press.

Jianguo, Yao. 1990. Beijing to host world ads meeting. *Beijing Review,* Oct. 1–7.

Johnson, Bradley. 1990. L.A. Catholic weeklies will vie for ad revenues. *Advertising Age,* Mar. 5.

Jones, Marsha. 1995. A critical and eclectic approach to media education: Overview of the Leicester workshop. *Media Development,* no. 2.

Kamakure, Wagner, and Thomas Novak. 1992. Value-system segmentation: Exploring the meaning of LOV. *Journal of Consumer Research,* no. 19.

Kavanaugh, John. 1983. Capitalist culture as a religious and educational formation system. *Religious Education* 78:1.

Keast, Ronald G. 1990. Vision TV: Canada's faith network goes it alone. *Media Development,* no. 4.

Keating, James. 1994. Initiation and moral education. *Church,* Summer.

Kelley, Dean. 1972. *Why Conservative Churches Are Growing.* New York: Harper and Row.

Kelly, Kevin. 1991. Chicago's Catholic Church: Putting its house in order. *Business Week,* June 10.

Kennedy, John. 1995. Redeeming the wasteland? *Christianity Today,* Oct. 2.

Kerr, Fergus. 1994. Frei's types. *New Blackfriars* 75:881.

Kirk, Jim. 1995. Vatican's worldly goodies. *Chicago Sun-Times,* Oct. 27.

Kuhn, Thomas. 1970. *The Structure of Scientific Revolutions,* 2nd edition. Chicago: University of Chicago Press.

Lane, Dermot, ed. 1986. *Religious Education and the Future.* Mahwah, N.J.: Paulist Press.

Langsdorf, Lenore. 1991. The emperor has only clothes: Toward a hermeneutic of the video text. In *Video Icons and Values*, eds. A. Olson, C. Parr, and D. Parr. Albany, N.Y.: SUNY Press.

Lee, Martyn J. 1993. *Consumer Culture Reborn: The Cultural Politics of Consumption*. London: Routledge.

Leiss, William, Stephen Kline, and Sut Jhally. 1990. *Social Communication in Advertising: Persons, Products & Images of Well-Being*, 2nd edition. New York: Routledge.

Levada, William J. 1996. Reflections on the age of confirmation. *Theological Studies*, no. 57.

Levine, Daniel H. 1992. *Popular Voices in Latin American Catholicism*. Princeton: Princeton University Press.

Lindbeck, George. 1984. *The Nature of Doctrine: Religion and Theology in a Postliberal Age*. Philadelphia: Fortress Press.

Lindsey, William D. 1995. Telling it slant: American Catholic public theology and prophetic discourse. *Horizons* 22:1.

Lints, Richard. 1993. The postpositivist choice: Tracy or Lindbeck. *Journal of the American Academy of Religion* 61: 4.

Lipietz, Alain. 1994. The national and the regional: Their autonomy vis-à-vis the capitalist world crisis. In *Transcending the State-Global Divide*, eds. R. Palan and B. Gills. Boulder: Lynne Rienner.

———— 1992. *Towards a New Economic Order: Postfordism, Ecology, and Democracy*. London: Oxford University Press.

———— 1987. *Miracles and Mirages: The Crisis of Global Fordism*. London: Verso.

Lipton, Michael. 1976. *Why Poor People Stay Poor: Urban Bias in World Development*. Cambridge: Harvard University Press.

Lohfink, Gerhard. 1984. *Jesus and Community: The Social Dimension of Christian Faith*. Philadelphia: Fortress Press.

Lohr, Steve. 1995. IBM to help Vatican open its archives to the computing masses. *New York Times*, Mar. 28.

Long, Karen R. 1994. Bible knowledge at record low, pollster says. *National Catholic Reporter*, July 15.

Loughlin, Gerard. 1996. *Telling God's Story: Bible, Church, and Narrative Theology*. Cambridge: Cambridge University Press.

Lukinsky, Joseph. 1993. Narratives and the program in religion and education. *Union Seminary Quarterly Review* 47:3–4.

Lyall, Sarah. 1994. A pope who is as prolific as he is high-priced. *New York Times*, July 20.

Lynch, Kevin. 1993. Reading numbers. *Church*, Winter.

MacIntyre, Alasdair. 1981, 1984. *After Virtue: A Study in Moral Theory*, 2nd edition. South Bend, Ind.: University of Notre Dame Press.

Maines, David. 1993. Narrative's moment and sociology's phenomena: Toward a narrative sociology. *Sociological Quarterly* 34:1.

Mallowe, Mike. 1994. Is your TV programming you? *U.S. Catholic* 59:3.

Malloy, Edward A. 1990. Church finances in crisis: How Catholic higher education can help. *America*, Sept. 1.

Malm, Krister, and Roger Wallis. 1992. *Media Policy & Music Activity*. London: Routledge.

Mandel, Ernest. 1975. *Late Capitalism*. London: NLB Books.

Marazziti, Mario. 1996. The charisma of the St. Egidio Community. *Origins* 26:5.

Marketing News. 1992. Mythologies can help build brands. Feb. 17.

_____ 1987. Third World research is difficult, but it's possible. Aug. 28.

Marriott, Robin. 1986. Ads require sensitivity to Arab culture, religion. *Marketing News*, Apr. 25.

Martin, James. 1994. Church TV. *America*, Nov. 5.

Masterman, Len. 1995. Media education worldwide: Objectives, values, and superhighways. *Media Development*, no. 2.

Mattelart, Armand. 1991. *Advertising International*. New York: Routledge.

May, Melanie. 1994. Replacing false images. *Media Development*, no. 2.

McDaniel, Colleen. 1995. *Material Christianity*. New Haven: Yale University Press.

McDaniel, James. 1989. The use of marketing techniques by churches: A national survey. *Review of Religious Research* 31:2.

_____ 1986. Church advertising: View of the clergy and general public. *Journal of Advertising* 15:1.

Media Development. 1995. Editorial. No. 2.

Menon, Vijay. 1993. Tradition meets modernity on the path to the global village. *Intermedia*, Jan.-Feb.

Meyrowitz, Joshua. 1985. *No Sense of Place: The Impact of Electronic Media on Social Behavior*. Oxford: Oxford University Press.

Miedema, Siebren. 1995. The quest for religious experience in education. *Religious Education* 90:3–4.

Milbank, John. 1991. The name of Jesus: Incarnation, atonement, ecclesiology. *Modern Theology* 7:4.

_____ 1990. *Theology and Social Theory*. London: Blackwell.

Ming, Li. 1991. International ad exhibition. *Beijing Review*, Mar. 18–24.

Mongovern, Anne Marie. 1992. Catechesis in the 90s: Present state and future challenges. *Chicago Studies* 31:2.

Moore, Joseph. 1994. Youth ministry: Redefining "Catholic identity." *Catholic World*, May-June.

Moore, R. Laurence. 1994. *Selling God: American Religion in the Marketplace of Culture*. Oxford: Oxford University Press.

Morey, Ann-Janine, and Todd Hedinger. 1996. Cornucopia kids and parents: Bowing down to mammon. *Christian Century*, Jan. 31.

Morgan, Michael. 1984. Television and democracy. In *Cultural Politics in Contemporary America*, eds. Ian Angus and Sut Jhally. London: Routledge.

Mowlana, Hamid. 1987. Mass media and culture: Toward an integrated theory. *Religious Education* 82:2.

Murphy, Craig N. 1996. Seeing women, recognizing gender, recasting international relations. *International Organization* 50:3.

Murray-Brown, Jeremy. 1991. Video ergo sum. In *Video Icons and Values*, eds. A. Olson, C. Parr, and D. Parr. Albany, N.Y.: SUNY Press.

Nash, Nathaniel. 1995. Group of 7 defines policies about telecommunications. *New York Times*, Feb. 27, p. C-1.

Navone, John. 1990. *Seeking God in Story*. Collegeville, Minn.: Liturgical Press.

Nelson, C. Ellis. 1993. Socialization revisited. *Union Seminary Quarterly Review* 47:3–4.

Neocatechumenate Movement. n.d. *In the Vatican*. Available from (http://www.catholic.net/RCC/Periodicals/Inside-0995/neocat1.html).

Newsweek. 1989. Help wanted: A few good fishers of men. June 26, p. 61.

New worlds to conquer. 1994. *Business Week*, Feb. 28, p. 50.

Niebuhr, Gustav. 1995. Religion journal: Taking on Hollywood, long before Dole. *New York Times*, sec. 1, p. 9.

———— 1991. Megachurches strive to be all things to all parishioners. *Wall Street Journal*, May 18.

Niebuhr, H. Richard. 1951. *Christ and Culture*. New York: Harper and Row.

Nussbaum, Martha. 1989. Narrative emotions: Beckett's genealogy of love. In *Why Narrative? Readings in Narrative Theology*, eds. Stanley Hauerwas and L. Gregory Jones. Grand Rapids, Mich.: Eerdmans.

Ochs, Peter, ed. 1993. *The Return to Scripture in Judaism and Christianity: Essays in Postcritical Scriptural Interpretation*. Mahwah, N.J.: Paulist Press.

O'Connor, James. 1973. *The Fiscal Crisis of the State*. New York: St. Martin's Press.

Offe, Claus. 1985. *Contradictions of the Welfare State*. Cambridge: MIT Press.

O'Keefe, Mary. 1995. The heart of Christian life: Conversion. *The Living Light* 31:4.

Olson, Alan. 1991. Video icons and values: An overview. In *Video Icons and Values*, eds. A. Olson, C. Parr and D. Parr. Albany, N.Y.: SUNY Press.

Olson, Alan, Christopher Parr, and Debra Parr, eds. 1991. *Video Icons and Values*. Albany, N.Y.: SUNY Press.

O'Malley, William J. 1992a. *Becoming a Catechist*. Mahwah, N.J.: Paulist Press.

———— 1992b. Understanding sacraments. *America*, Mar. 7.

———— 1991. Emergent adults and self-esteem. *America*, Jan. 19.

———— 1990a. *Converting the Baptized: A Survival Manual for Parents, Teachers, and Pastors*. Allen, Tex.: Tabor Publishing.

_____ 1990b. The Peter Pan syndrome. *America*, Sept. 22.

_____ 1990c. Placebo Christianity. *America*, Apr. 14.

_____ 1990d. Parents are apostles. *America*, Jan. 20.

Orsi, Michael P. 1994. Catechesis in the third millennium. *Religious Education* 89:3.

Ott, Richard. 1992. *Creating Demand*. Burr Ridge, Ill.: Irwin Professional Publishing.

Paden, William. 1992. *Interpreting the Sacred: Ways of Viewing Religion*. Boston: Beacon Press.

Palan, Ronen, and Barry Gills, eds. 1994. *Transcending the State-Global Divide*. Boulder: Lynne Rienner Publishers.

Parsons, Paul. 1993. While in China, advertising blooms like a thousand flowers. *Advertising Age*, July 19.

Parsons, Susan. 1995. Feminist ethics after modernity: Towards an appropriate universalism. *Studies in Christian Ethics* 8:1.

PASCH (Parishioners Against a Secret Church). Documents at (http://out-world.compuserve.com/homepages/Ronald_Haynes/).

Peck, Jamie, and Adam Tickell. 1994. Searching for a new institutional fix: The after-Fordist crisis and the global-local disorder. In *Post-Fordism*, ed. Ash Amin. Oxford: Blackwell.

Perrin, Robin, and Armand Mauss. 1993. Strictly speaking: Kelley's quandary and the Vineyard Christian Fellowship. *Journal for the Scientific Study of Religion* 32:2.

Peterson, Anna L. 1996. Religious narratives and political protest. *Journal of the American Academy of Religion* 64:1.

Pieris, Aloysius. 1995. Whither new evangelism? *The Month*, November.

Piirto, Rebecca. 1991. *Beyond Mind Games: The Marketing Power Psychographics*. Ithaca: American Demographics Books.

Piore, Michael, and Charles Sabel. 1984/1994. *The Second Industrial Divide*. New York: Basic Books.

Piveteau, Didier. 1986. School, society, and catechesis. In *Religious Education and the Future*, ed. Dermot Lane. Mahwah, N.J.: Paulist Press.

Poewe, Karla. 1994. *Charismatic Christianity as a Global Culture*. Columbia, S.C.: University of South Carolina Press.

Pope John Paul II. 1996. Penitential fasting is therapy for the soul. *L'Osservatore Romano*, Mar. 13, p. 1.

_____ 1995. Ecclesia in Africa (Apostolic Exhortation). *Origins* 25:16.

_____ 1994. Television and the family: Guidelines for good viewing (Message for 1994 World Communications Day, May 15). Obtained from Paul Halsall (Halsall@murray.fordham.edu).

_____ 1991. Redemptoris Missio. *Origins* 20:34.

_____ 1979. Redemptor Hominis. *Origins* 19.

Pope, Stanley J. 1993. The "preferential option for the poor": An ethic for "saints and heroes"? *Irish Theological Quarterly* 59:3.

Portes, Alejandro, Manuel Castells, and Laura Benton. 1989. *The Informal Economy: Studies in Advanced and Less Developed Countries.* Baltimore: Johns Hopkins University Press.

Postman, Neil. 1985. *Amusing Ourselves to Death.* New York: Penguin.

Proudfood, Wayne. 1985. *Religious Experience.* Berkeley: University of California
Press.

Pungente, John. 1996. Windows on the landscape: Taking television seriously.
(Available from pungente@epas.utoronto.ca)

————— 1994. Live long and prosper: Media literacy in the USA. *Clipboard* 8:2.
(Available from pungente@epas.utoronto.ca)

————— 1993. Signs and symbols of the transcendent: Revisiting our media environment. Jesuit Communication Project. (Available from pungente@epas.
utoronto.ca)

————— n.d. The second spring: Media education in Canada's secondary schools.
(Available at pungente@epas.utoronto.ca)

Quester, George. 1990. *The International Politics of Television.* Lexington, Mass.:
Lexington Books.

Rabinow, Paul. 1984. Introduction to *The Foucault Reader,* ed. Paul Rabinow.
New York: Pantheon.

Reeves, Geoffrey. 1993. *Communications and the "Third World."* London: Routledge.

Religious News Service. 1994. Merchandiser adds suit to World Youth Day sou-
venir flap. *Chicago Tribune,* Aug. 19.

Roebben, Bert. 1995. Do we still have faith in young people? A West-European
answer to the evangelization of young people in a postmodern world. *Religious
Education* 90:3–4.

Rohr, Richard. 1994. The goal of Christian ministry. *Catholic World* 237:1421.

Ross, Robert J. S., and Kent Trachte. 1990. *Global Capitalism.* Albany, N.Y.:
SUNY Press.

Rossi, Philip, and Paul Soukup, eds. 1994. *Mass Media and the Moral Imagination.*
Kansas City: Sheed & Ward.

Sarno, Ronald. 1992. Steps to television awareness and appreciation. In *Media and
Culture,* ed. Reynolds Ekstrom. New Rochelle, N.Y.: Don Bosco/Multimedia.

————— 1987. *Using Media in Religious Education.* Birmingham, Ala.: Religious
Education Press.

Savan, Leslie. 1994. *The Sponsored Life.* Philadelphia: Temple University Press.

Schiller, Herbert I. 1994. Media, technology and the market: The interacting dynamic. In *Culture on the Brink: Ideologies of Technology,* eds. Gretchen Bender
and Timothy Drucker. Seattle: Bay Press.

————— 1989. *Culture, Inc.: The Corporate Takeover of Public Expression.* New York:
Oxford University Press.

Schodolski, Vincent, and Gary Dretzka. 1995. A world of interest in media deals.
Chicago Tribune, Aug. 6.

Scholes, Robert. 1991. Power and pleasure in video texts. In *Video Icons and Values*, eds. A. Olson, C. Parr, and D. Parr. Albany, N.Y.: SUNY Press.

Schor, Juliet. 1991. *The Overworked American*. New York: Basic Books.

Schudson, Michael. 1984. *Advertising: The Uneasy Persuasion*. New York: Basic Books.

Shao, Alan, and John Hill. 1992. Executing transnational advertising campaigns: Do U.S. agencies have the overseas talent? *Journal of Advertising Research*, Jan.-Feb.

Shayon, Robert Lewis, and Nash Cox. 1994. *Religion, Television, and the Information Superhighway: Conference Report*. Philadelphia: Waymark Press.

Sidey, Ken. 1991. Church growth fine tunes its formulas. *Christianity Today*, June 24.

Simon, Michael A. 1982. *Understanding Human Action*. Albany, N.Y.: SUNY Press.

Sinclair, John, Elizabeth Jacka, and Stuart Cunningham. 1996. *New Patterns in Global Television: Peripheral Vision*. London: Oxford University Press.

Sloan, Douglas. 1993. Religious education and the evolution of consciousness. *Union Seminary Quarterly Review* 47:3–4.

Smart, Brian. 1986. The politics of truth and the problem of hegemony. In *Foucault: A Critical Reader*, ed. D. C. Hoy. Oxford: Blackwell.

Smith, Anthony. 1991. *The Age of Behemoths: The Globalization of Mass Media Firms*. New York: A Twentieth Century Fund Paper/Priority Press.

Smith, Harmon L. 1995. *Where Two or More Are Gathered: Liturgy and the Moral Life*. Cleveland: Pilgrim Press.

Smith, Joanmarie. 1994. Teaching toward conversion. *Religious Education* 89:1.

Smith, Wilfred Cantwell. 1963. *The Meaning and End of Religion*. New York: Harper & Row.

Smolowe, Jill. 1990. Read this. *Time*, Nov. 26.

Sobrino, Jon. 1987. *Jesus in Latin America*. Maryknoll, N.Y.: Orbis Books.

_____ 1978. *Christology at the Crossroads*. Maryknoll, N.Y.: Orbis Books.

Soskice, Janet. 1995. Community and morality "after modernity": A response to Robin Gill. *Studies in Christian Ethics* 8:1.

Soukup, Paul. 1993. Church documents and the media. In *Mass Media*, eds. J. Coleman and M. Tomka. *Concilium*, no. 5.

Soukup, Paul, Frances Ford Plude, and Paul Philbert. 1995. A dialogue on communication and theology. *New Theology Review* 8:4.

Spielvogel, Carl. 1991. The Americas. *Vital Speeches*, Nov. 15.

Spohn, William C. 1994. Notes on moral theology: Jesus and Christian ethics. *Theological Studies*, no. 56.

_____ 1990. The moral vision of the catechism: Thirty years that did not happen. *America*, Mar. 3.

Star TV rising. 1993. *The Economist*, Apr. 17.

Stassen, Glen. 1994. Narrative justice as reiteration. In *Theology Without Foundations*, eds. S. Hauerwas, N. Murphy, and M. Nation. Nashville, Tenn.: Abingdon.

Steele, Richard. 1994. Narrative theology and the religious affections. In *Theology Without Foundations*, eds. S. Hauerwas, N. Murphy, and M. Nation. Nashville, Tenn.: Abingdon.

Stell, Stephen L. 1993. Hermeneutics in theology and the theology of hermeneutics: Beyond Lindbeck and Tracy. *Journal of the American Academy of Religion* 61:4.

Stern, Aimee. 1986. Public service pays off for ad agencies. *Dun's Business Month*, June.

Sterngold, James. 1992. The awakening Chinese consumer. *New York Times*, Oct. 11, p. F-1.

Stewart, Thomas. 1989. Turning around the Lord's business. *Fortune*, Sept. 25.

Strate, Lance. 1991. The cultural meaning of beer commercials. *Advances in Consumer Research*, no. 18.

Stross, Randall. 1990. The return of advertising in China: A survey of the ideological reversal. *China Quarterly*, September.

Sweetser, Thomas P. 1990. The parish of the future: Beyond the programs. *America*, Mar. 10.

Tagliabue, John. 1995. At Vatican Library, computers join Middle Ages. *New York Times*, May 1.

_____ 1994. Publishers push a book by the pope. *New York Times*, Oct. 20.

Television in Latin America. 1993. *Intermedia*, Aug.-Sept., nos. 4–5.

Television's final frontier. 1993. *The Economist*, July 31.

Thistlewaite, Susan. 1996. A Schliermacher for our time: A review of David Tracy's *On Naming the Present: God, Hermeneutics, and Church*. *Theology Today* 53:2.

Thompson, John B. 1990. *Ideology and Modern Culture*. Stanford: Stanford University Press.

Tilley, Terrence W. 1995. *Postmodern Theologies: The Challenge of Religious Diversity*. Maryknoll, N.Y.: Orbis Books.

Tracy, David. 1994. Literary theory and the return of the forms for naming and thinking God in theology. *Journal of Religion* 74:3.

Troeltsch, Ernst. 1913/1981. *The Social Teachings of the Christian Churches*, vols. 1–2. Chicago: University of Chicago Press.

Tse, David, Russell Belk, and Nan Zhou. 1989. Becoming a consumer society: A longitudinal and cross-cultural content analysis of print ads from Hong Kong, the People's Republic of China, and Taiwan. *Journal of Consumer Research*, no. 15.

Tunstall, Jeremy, and Michael Palmer. 1991. *Media Moguls*. London: Routledge.

United States Catholic Conference. 1986. *In the Sight of All. Communications: A Vision All Can Share*. Washington, D.C.: USCC.

Vale, Norman. 1992. Advertising post-1992: A threat to Euromarketing? *International Advertiser* 4:1.

Verbeke, William. 1992. Advertisers do not persuade consumers: They create societies around their brands to maintain power in the marketplace. *International Journal of Advertising* 1:1.

Veverka, Fayette Breaux. 1993. Re-imagining Catholic identity: Toward an analogical paradigm of religious education. *Religious Education* 88:2.

Von Wright, G. H., and Heikki Nyman, eds. 1980. *Culture and Value*. Chicago: University of Chicago Press.

Waide, John. 1987. The making of self and world in advertising. *Journal of Business Ethics*, no. 6.

Walker, Don. 1993. Media literacy: The Vatican echoes McLuhan. *America*, Mar. 6.

Walker, R. B. J. 1992. *Inside/Outside: International Relations as Political Theory*. Cambridge: Cambridge University Press.

Wallerstein, Immanuel. 1991. *Geopolitics and Geoculture*. Cambridge: Cambridge University Press.

Wangensteen, Betsy. 1996. Archdiocese turnaround. *Crain's Chicago Business*, Jan. 15–21.

Warren, Michael. 1997. Decisions that pattern, patterns that decide. In *Paths That Lead to Life: The Church as Counterculture*, eds. Michael L. Budde and Robert Brimlow. Forthcoming from SUNY Press.

———. 1995. Life structure or the material conditions of living: An ecclesial task. *New Theology Review* 8:4.

———. 1994a. Judging the electronic communications media. *The Living Light* 31:2.

———. 1994b. The sacramentality of critique and its challenge to Christian educators. *Christian Education Journal* 15:1.

———. 1993. Religious education and the task of cultural critique. *Religious Education* 88:1.

———. 1992. *Communications and Cultural Analysis: A Religious View*. Westport, Conn.: Bergin & Garvey.

———. 1989. *Faith, Culture, and the Worshiping Community: Shaping the Practice of the Local Church*. Mahwah, N.J.: Paulist Press.

———. 1988a. Youth and emerging commitments: Toward a catechesis of wealth. *Youth Ministry Resource Network Occasional Paper*. Naugatuck, Conn.: Center for Ministry Development.

———. 1988b. The electronically imagined world and religious education. *Religious Education* 83:3.

———. 1987a. Religious formation in the context of social formation. *Religious Education* 82:4.

———. 1987b. Images and the structuring of experience. *Religious Education* 82:2.

Wasko, Janet. 1994. *Hollywood in the Information Age*. Austin, Tex.: University of Texas Press.

Webber, Robert, and Rodney Clapp. 1988. *People of the Truth*. Harrisburg, Penn.: Morehouse Publishing.

Weber, Max. 1963. *The Sociology of Religion*. Boston: Beacon Press.

_____ 1905. *The Protestant Ethic and the Spirit of Capitalism*. Boston: Beacon Press.

Wentz, Laurel. 1990. Call it Catholic aid. *Advertising Age* Apr. 9.

White, Gayle. 1991. Ministry meets Madison Ave.: Churches sold on marketing. *Atlanta Journal-Constitution*, Nov. 3.

White, Susan J. 1994. *Christian Worship and Technological Change*. Nashville, Tenn.: Abingdon.

Willimon, William H. 1995. Christian ethics: When the personal is political is cosmic. *Theology Today* 52:3.

Wong, Jesse. 1993. Star TV views China as a big market, but Murdoch may get poor reception. *Wall Street Journal*, Sept. 14, p. A-17.

Wuthnow, Robert. 1994. What religious people think about the poor. *Christian Century*, Sept. 7–14.

_____ 1993. Pious materialism. *Christian Century*, Mar. 3.

Yamane, David, and Megan Polzer. 1994. Ways of seeing ecstacy in modern society: Experiential-expressive and cultural-linguistic views. *Sociology of Religion* 55:1.

Yates, Ronald E. 1994. A.C. Nielson grabs Asian data giant that IRI had sought. *Chicago Tribune*, July 9.

Yoder, John Howard. 1994. *The Royal Priesthood: Essays Ecclesiological and Ecumenical*. Grand Rapids, Mich.: Eerdmans.

Yu, Shuang. 1992. Ads lead China into consumers' era. *Beijing Review*, Feb. 24–Mar. 1.

Zhou, Nan, and Russell W. Belk. 1993. China's advertising and the export marketing learning curve: The first decade. *Journal of Advertising Research*, Nov.-Dec.

Zukowski, Angela Ann. 1993a. Children and television. *Catholic World*, Nov.-Dec.

_____ 1993b. Should the Mass be televised? *America*, Apr. 17.

About the Book and Author

In *The (Magic) Kingdom of God*, Michael Budde offers a multidisciplinary analysis of the "global culture industries"—increasingly powerful, centralized corporate conglomerates in television, advertising, marketing, movies, and the like—and their impact on Christian churches in industrialized countries. Utilizing ideas from contemporary and classical schools of political economy, the author explains why the study of global culture industries is essential for understanding the current era of global capitalism.

In suggesting that the cultural ecology shaped by these industries undermines many of the primary processes and structures through which people become committed Christians, Budde offers a novel utilization of linguistic-based theories of religious formation. Responses by churches to the new situation—more religious education or attempts to use the global culture industries for Christian purposes—are explored and found lacking. For the subversive praxis of Jesus of Nazareth to endure in the cultural ecology of postmodernism, Budde argues, churches must come to embrace their role as radical and countercultural alternative communities in which lay formation becomes a central preoccupation.

Michael Budde is associate professor of political science at DePaul University.

Index

Sacramental liberalism, 98–100
Saint Therese, 4
San Egidio Community, 137–138
Schiller, Herbert, 33
Schuller, Robert, 114
Scripture study, 127, 137, 138. *See also*
    Narrative theology
Searle, Mark, 144
Sects, 7–8
Secularization, 71–72
Separatism, 140
Service, 3, 134, 137, 148
Sheila-ism, 87
Signorelli, Nancy, 74
Simmel, Georg, 37
Smith, Anthony, 30–31
Smith, Harmon, 142, 143
Sobrino, Jon, 66
Social engagement, 112, 144–150
Social good, 6–7, 64
Social Teaching of the Christian Churches,
    The (Troeltsch), 7
Society, effect on church, 144
Soskice, Janet, 64
Spain, 139, 140
Spirituality, 147
SRC. *See* Survey Research Group
Stassen, Glen, 63, 64
State, 19, 145. *See also* Political practice
Steele, Richard B., 62
Sterngold, James, 51
Sullivan, Barry, 112
Survey Research Group (SRC), 46
Symbols, 59, 65, 90–94
    fragmentation of, 36, 44

Taxation, 109, 112
TCI (media corporation), 110
Tele-evangelism, 111–112
Television, 70–82
    accessibility of, 76–77
    cable, 110–111
    in China, 47–48
    decontextualization in, 80, 85–86
    deregulation of, 29, 31, 79
    fragmentation in, 77, 80

and lived experience, 78
multicultural networks, 120–121
privatization of, 79
programming in, 79–80
and reciprocal effect of societal factors,
    74–75
religious symbols in advertising, 90–94
spin-off products, 80
structure of, 75–78, 80, 85–86
viewing habits, 73–74, 77, 78, 82–84
visuality, 75, 76
See also Advertising; Culture industries
Testimonials of faith, 128
Theology and Social Theory (Milbank), 13
Things of the Spirit (John Paul II), 107
Third World. *See* Economic development
    policy
Thompson, J. Walter (advertising firm),
    34, 35
Tickell, Adam, 24
Tillich, Paul, 17
Tilly, Terence, 63
Time-Warner (media conglomerate),
    29–30, 31
Tracy, David, 55–56, 63
Troeltsch, Ernst, 7

United Kingdom, 34, 140
University of Chicago, 55
Urbanization, 52

Vatican Library, 106
Vatican Radio, 108
VISION TV, 120–121
VISN. *See* Faith and Values Network

Wallerstein, Immanuel, 17
Walzer, Michael, 63, 64
Warren, Michael, 128, 131–133, 135, 141,
    142, 147
Way, The (Neocatechumenate
    Movement), 139
Webber, Robert, 147
Weber, Max, 7
Weber, Robert, 143
White, Gayle, 113–114

Stained glass piece. ? (cost)